D1414361

Pieces of Eight

FIRST EDITION

Copyright © 1992 Wordsmith Publishing Inc.^{TM}

All Rights Reserved

Manufactured in The United States of America

ISBN 0-9628611-7-0

Library of Congress Catalog Card Number: 92-80989

For information write, Wordsmith Publishing, Inc. ^{TM}
6100 Longmeadow Blvd. S. Saginaw, Michigan 48603

Type composition and electronic paste-ups by
Rotesch Graphics,^{TM} Saginaw, Michigan

Section I
The Graduating Class of 1922
Bettye K. Wray

Section II
The Good Earth
Robert W. Bennett

Section III
Transformation
Kathleen Lee Mendel

Section IV
1 on 1
Laurence W. Thomas

Section V
Season's End
Denise Martinson

Section VI
Meditated Solitude
Patrick Pillars

Section VII
After the Rain Comes the Rainbow
Rosemary J. Schmidt

Section VIII
Passepartout Chanson
Christopher Corbett-Fiacco

We dedicate this book to all who enjoy poetry

Robert W. Bennett

Christopher Albert Pierce

Patrick Villars

Laurence W. Thomas

Denise Martinson

Kathleen Lee Mendel

Rosemary J. Schmidt

Bettye K. Wray

INTRODUCTION

On the kind invitation of fellow-poet and editor, Rosemary J. Schmidt, am I happy to write in behalf of Pieces of Eight, a sheaf of poetry I deem uniquely qualified for high regard for its literary and poetic insights.

It would be easy to make comments about the work included of individual poets; but instead I prefer to deal with the volume as a whole, gestaltistically, holistically. For, as I see it, we poets ought not to compete with each other; instead we should complement each other's efforts recognizing that we are not competitors, none better or less so, just different, each with our individual abilities and responsive- ness to express ideas spontaneously in his/her own milieu and verbal approach.

As I read through the book in galley, here and there I was deeply struck by the very intensity of the poets' overall substance and qualities and insights. Witness such beauty as "I'd brave a bushelful of thorns/ for a petal/ of your love"; "friendship is sanctuary/ not shelter"; "There are no distant drums beating./ The strife is here/ On this battlefield now."; "'The Lord is by our side'", said one of them./ Another said, 'We are men'"; "For now, we teach/ these flightless birds fly-/ to wherever their wings take them"; "And the north winds blow/ through the field and hill,/ and the elms cry softly/ of the winter's dying years".

And there are more, many more beautiful lines and phraseology and insights and feelings, poignant and succinct, sublime and sound. The poets represented in Pieces of Eight are with a message: of hope, of sense, of rationality, of meaningfulness in living. While the disclosures of their poetic lines have an originality to them to engage one's intellect, they possess a beauty to satisfy the moral nature. They have passed the governing thought in their poems back and forth through the refining stones of the mill of reflection.

The poets write with feeling and being-ness in truthfulness --- one of purest and simplest of poetical themes, if accomplished honestly and without flourish. They strive to embrace a different, even a differing consciousness, a greater awareness, of life.

I have always felt that poetry depends on the writer's character and temperament. For poetry --- the art of solitude --- requires a great deal of thought and all the sincerity of which a person's nature is capable.

In Pieces of Eight the lines so very often share our hopes, fears, angers and struggles of the prosaic world. They have searched for truths rather than of sweet truisms.

In my own work I have written that poetry is an argument of today and a hint of tomorrow. Poets have an obligation to express a sense of the universal. If they serve only a singular purpose, poets are the unconscious heralds of larger dispensations. Our poetry, if it is to be successful, is a representation of an idea, with originality energized in the world of beauty, truly a treatise of our existence.

Pieces of Eight accomplishes two main functions of poetry: to transfuse emotion and to transmit thought. This little volume contains moods and views vital and dynamic. It further establishes the thesis that the province of poetry is the entire range of human experience and that vast area of moral destiny.

As a behavioral scientist and poetry therapist, as well as a practitioner in the art of poetry, I recommend Pieces of Eight for its encompassing and consistent effort to give values to life. Essentially, our holistic education develops mind, body, emotions, imagination, intuition, and man's spirit. The impact of poetry to be found in Pieces of Eight espouses a core wherein our polarities of feeling are synthesized into an entity.

West Orange, New Jersey
  May - 1992

Hirsch Lazaar Silverman, Ph.D., D.Sc., LL.D., D.H.L., Litt.D., is a Fellow of the World Academy of Poets, a member of the Academy of American Poets and the New Jersey Poetry Society (of which he is a Past Trustee), a Fellow of the World Academy of Arts and Sciences: author of 17 books, including 7 volumes of poetry, and contributor of articles to over 140 journals nationally and internationally; a member of the National Advisory Board of the Poetry Therapy Institute; a Founder Fellow of the International Academy of Poets. He is also a member of The Royal Society of Literature, and a Benjamin Franklin Fellow of the Royal Society of Arts, of England. Dr. Silverman is a Fellow of the World Poetry Society and the United Poets Laureate International; and holds Diplomate status as International Eminent Poet by the International Poets Academy. He is an elected member of The Poetry Society of America; and is both a Certified and Registered Poetry Therapist of the National Association of Poetry Therapy. Hirsch Lazaar Silverman is the awardee of Diplomat in Poetry with Laureate Honors by the UPLI; and is the recipient of the first annual Creative Leadership Award of Kappa Delta Pi of New York University.

Pieces of Eight

Editor: Rosemary J. Schmidt

Wordsmith Publishing Inc.
Saginaw, Michigan

The Graduating Class of 1922

Bettye K. Wray

About the Author

BETTYE K. WRAY was born and raised in Birmingham, Alabama. For a period of twenty years, she lived in New York. Today she lives in Birmingham, returning there after the death of her husband. She is the founder of **K-Wray Publications, Poet's Newsletter** and **Dear Magnolia.** Bettye states that being an editor of a poetry publication is the answer to a dream. Writing since grammar school days, she believes it is a great privilege to be in contact with poets and that each of them has a contribution to the art. She firmly believes that the creative art of writing is a gift that can be improved upon with work and education. The seed, she states, was inside a poet and through their efforts they made the flowers grow and fulfilled their talent.

Her poetry has appeared in numerous publications, including *Negative Capability, Amelia, Voices International, Piedmont Literary Review, Quarter Moon, Broken Streets, Stand* (England), *Arby's National Newsletter, Happiness Magazine,* among others. In 1989 she was selected to be included in a hardcover book, <u>An Alabama Scrapbook</u>, a collection of 31 contributors who grew up in Alabama.

Bettye believes there is poetry in each day. She is constantly looking for it.

CONTENTS

SITTING ON THE STEPS OF ARLINGTON _____ 2
THE TIN CUP BRIGADE MARCHES
                ON THE FOURTH OF JULY _____ 3
GRANDPA LANE _____ 4
THE GRADUATING CLASS OF 1922 _____ 5
DEPRESSION IN RECESSION _____ 6
A TRIBUTE TO CRAZY HORSE _____ 7
A SEARCH FOR RED CLOUD'S LOVE _____ 7
INDIAN HARVEST_____ 8
ARIZONA REFLECTIONS _____ 9
DAMIEN, LEPER PRIEST _____ 10
A CLOWN _____ 11
BRIEF ENCOUNTER WITH DISMAL SWAMP _____ 12
THE SUICIDE OF ANNE SEXTON _____ 13
DALMATIAN TRIPTYCH _____ 14
ANSWER TO SYLVIA PLATT_____ 15
RETURN TO WALES _____ 16
WELSH MINER _____ 17
I WILL CRY IN AUGUST _____ 19
FAIR FINALE _____ 20
WINTER PRELUDE _____ 21
PRELUDE TO THE NURSING HOME _____ 21
THE BRACELET _____ 22
AN AGING ACTRESS PREPARES
                FOR HER OSCAR-WINNING ROLE _____ 23
TWILIGHT WALTZING _____ 24
THE WAR TO END ALL WARS _____ 24

SITTING ON THE STEPS OF ARLINGTON
(An Ante-bellum Home)

Sitting on the steps of Arlington,
wearing jogging shoes, shirt and jeans.
Looking across the wide lawn
where memory rides the old streetcar
traveling down Tuscaloosa Avenue.
Thoughts wander inside Elyton Grammar School
where young girls walk down the halls
in rustling taffeta dresses--
velvet ribbons in their hair.
Listening to choir-voices
drifting from inside Walker Memorial Church
in perfect harmony.

Long past--
Arlington at Christmas time;
walking on plush carpet
inside the parlor room
where the huge Yule tree,
beside the Steinway piano,
sparkled like a Swiss village
vision from Heidi Land.

May I go inside?
I'll wear an evening dress and pearls--
golden party shoes.

Sitting on the steps of Arlington,
looking back to goodbye.

THE TIN CUP BRIGADE MARCHES
ON THE FOURTH OF JULY

The congregation sang Fa Sol La
inside the wooden frame Southern Church.
In nineteen thirty-six the heat
pressed heavily like a coffin lid.

Young wives sang soprano and alto
in homemade harmony; some held infants
who had not faced winter.
Old women who had known all seasons
lifted high-pitched voices.
Men, wearing white shirts and black ties,
voiced like thunder, but brought
no heavenly rain.

Little children, asleep on church pews,
awakened and went outside
to parade up a little hill behind the church
that led to cool spring water.
They took little tin cups with them
and drank of the refreshing goodness.

Inside the church
they sang Fa Sol La--
pleading for mercy.

4

To each man is given a marble to carve for the wall:
A stone that is needed to heighten the beauty of all;
And only his soul has the magic to give it a grace:
And only his hands have the cunning to put it in place
-- Edwin Markham

GRANDPA LANE

Grandpa's farmhous nestled at the end
of the light-filtered lane.
We would toot the old Buick
up Horseshoe Bend
to announce we were almost there.
He was always waiting on the porch
near where wisteria bloomed
at its time to bloom.

Grandpa built my best swing,
with ropes so long,
I felt I could sail the sky --
over the ash-hopper and smokehouse.
He gave me Sears Robuck catalogues
from which I cut paperdoll families,
and peppermint candy pieces that
came from the coffee bean can.

In the early evenings,
standing at his lift-top desk,
he would read to the family:
Mother, Aunt Louva, Aunt Mary
R. L., Roy, Martha, Barbara and me --
child and grandchild alike.

Behind his desk a map of the United States
with bordered photographs of the presidents
up to Woodrow Wilson.
I can hear Seth Thomas on the mantel
above the fireplace tick his life still.
And see, beside his desk,
his mother's old trunk that held treasures
of well-worn marbles, granite white,
a quilt she had made, baby shoes,
and several little girl bonnets.

Near his life's end, I would be the one
to read to him: Dear Abby.
Grandpa was quite a man.
He died at 93.

THE GRADUATING CLASS OF 1922

Four girls and one boy.
Standing outside the old
country schoolhouse, the
photograph was made
before they left --
seeking tomorrow.

The boy died on the last day
of World War II.
One girl died when her child
was born in 1924.
Another died in an automobile
that hit a train in 1928.
One died of pneumonia
in 1929.

One was mother.
The angels came for her
when she was eighty
as she sat in her rocking chair
crocheting little doilies.

DEPRESSION IN RECESSION
(After the Steelmills Closed)

A fatality is their love, buried in reflections
of the yellow house in Bessemer.
He departed toward a place called nowhere,
looking for somewhere.
Alone, he drove over the Mary Susan Bryant Bridge.
She is back there in her world without togetherness
where only idle dreams remain replacing smiling faces
of once new morning suns.
Sunset sky glows across the path of fading day;
gone the hello of yesterday, he travels the presence
of today's goodbye into the unknown darkness
of tomorrow where the moon no longer climbs the sky
and southern stars no longer flame.
On each side he views the still-life
of unemployment. The now idle smokestacks
of Fairfield are desolate, cold.
Once those furnaces were life, like bodies,
warm and fulfilled;
now they hunger, the not knowing yet.
Today there is only depression in recession.
Nothing leads to the way they were.

A TRIBUTE TO CRAZY HORSE

Tashunkewitka, known as Crazy Horse,
A living portrait - you - in fringed attire
With eagle-feathered bonnet, proudly worn.
Were you not sad when dust of death's cold wind
Blew chill across your heart for pale-face foe?
Where white man fell a silence now prevails.
Well, Custer won the glory that he craved;
His ghost remains forever now at large
While Little Big Horn has sad memories.
And freedom came at last to Crazy Horse
Who rides in sculpture through Dakota Hills.
I wonder yet, what did it really prove?

A SEARCH FOR RED CLOUD'S LOVE

Where lies the maiden who was Red Cloud's love?
The Great Souix Chief who left his mark on life
And death on grasslands of Montana's soil.
Perhaps she sleeps where winds blow fierce across
The plains, there where the buffalo once roamed.
Or does her greening shawl of earth protect
In Rocky Mountain's vast and peaceful land?
And did she know before she went to sleep,
A sweeping bath of lovelight from dark eyes,
And tender kisses from the warring Chief?
Please tell her name, where does she rest in peace,
And where are the children that they left behind?

Among great souls who soar in skies beyond,
Is Red Cloud there forever with his love?

INDIAN HARVEST

In the moon of the cherries blossoming
after the sun sweeps snow from the earth,
And after we swim in waters that fall
like tears down our sacred mountains;
When pasques blush and hold hands
with green grass when warm breezes stir,
we plant the seed.

As the corn grows tall, we will rest
on mossy places at the roadsides with
old squaws and sell Indian trinkets --
moccasins, beads, feathered headdress
copied from one worn by Looking Glass,
replicas of Indians made of wood --
some tiny Navajo dolls.

When harvesting, we will hear nothing
but the caws of birds and the moans
of old Chiefs rattling tired bones.
Then, in the moon of the first snow falling,
Covered by a thin blanket of survival,
we sleep again.

Wah-Kon-Tah, Great Spirit,
look down upon us
and be pleased.

ARIZONA REFLECTIONS

Silence in Canyon de Chelly.
Intense backlighting at setting sun
of cottonwood and sycamore
with rich hue of sandstone
reflects like a breathtaking mirror
in a meandering stream.

We whisper.

Anaszi tribe spirits caress
the moment -- ancient ones
here before the Navajo.
Hoof sounds of Kit Carson's invading army
echo in time;
neither they nor the Navajo
claim this paradise.

We whisper.

Golden tones everywhere
suggests brightness
of eternal light.
The moon will illuminate dark stillness,
the wind travel gently toward a place
we do not know
leaving thoughts of Eden.

We whisper.

DAMIEN, LEPER PRIEST

Ah, Damien, you came from Tremeloo,
A town in Belgium's safe and thriving land
Where windmills turned in rippling fields of wheat.
You could not turn your thoughts from Molokai,
The Sandwich Islands, palmed and flower-strewn,
Where first you walked fair Puno's lonely roads
And gazed upon the roofs where blossoms hung
In splendor -- hues of purple, red, and maize.
Dear Father, Kamiano, there you stayed,
Forever in your place in Molokai.
You entered the enclosure joining those
In saddened state -- despair and deepest pain.
They sang their native tunes and smiled and prayed
Beneath white clouds that played in skies of blue.
You gave a life of service for the One
Who died so tragic on the tree for you.

The ocean waves still thunder on that shore,
Just as your voice broke silence long ago.
"We lepers," meaning all, are one, you said,
In that arena with the purest white.
Ah, Damien, we thank you for your light!

A CLOWN

Poet, don't fall in love
with that poet. Become invisible.
Watch. Hide in the closet.
Look out the keyhole
with yearning, hungry eyes.
See how cozy and content
the other poet appears
sitting before the fireplace.
Is the heart reading aloud
with no voice? See how
the dog gets a pat on the head.
The soft breeze whispering
outside in the pine trees
is a gentle message for you:
Lock the closet door.
The dog was once a poet.
You say: It is too late,
the lock is broken;
You are not really a poet,
only a clown.

BRIEF ENCOUNTER WITH DISMAL SWAMP
(SE Virginia and NE South Carolina near the Chesapeake Bay)

With eerie lights and wraith-like silhouettes,
The swamp held legends, wild and weird and strange.
Ascending veils of mist laced through the dark;
A place no human being should invade.
But Poet Robert Frost, at eighteen years,
Proceeded in to lose himself and die
In Dismal Swamp, because of long-lost love.
He sought dark tunnels closed by ancient trees,
And looked for traps of doom that snared and killed.
He did not die, instead he found safe lights
Where hosts of iridescent butterflies
Bathed in fragrant rarest jessamine
And eglantine and laurel spiced with rose.
He was set free by Dismal Swamp
To swing on birches under diamond stars,
And receive world acclaim awaiting him.

THE SUICIDE OF ANNE SEXTON

Anne, you did not need to go.
Robins still sing in the Spring.
Winter has its first virgin snow.
The sun is shining today.

What did you learn?
What did you see
Still unrevealed to the likes of me?
I know a light guides me on;
What did you see in your light,
A Lorelei's song?

Perhaps it was an illusion,
Your conclusion.
You did not get away, you know.
I am reading your poetry today.

DALMATIAN TRIPTYCH

"...I come with kisses in my hood
and the sun, the smart one,
rolling in my arms.
So I say Live
and turn my shadow three times around
to feed our puppies as they come,
the eight Dalmatians we didn't drown
despite the warnings..."

-- Anne Sexton
"Live" in
Live or Die

I.

On the plane flight to the city
she held carefully
a fancy-wrapped package
containing two ceramic dalmatian dogs
she made for him two years before
when first the trip was planned.
After time passed
and him two lovers later,
he would be waiting to welcome her
when she arrived at last.

II.

The rosewood coffee table
stands in the parlor room
near the west window,
sunlight streaming across its surface
until evening shadows fall.
Near the center are two ceramic dalmatian dogs,
made for a friend who is no longer a friend.

III.

The ghosts of lovers
haunt the side streets of New York
walking Dot and Spot
in the no longer virgin snow.

ANSWER TO SYLVIA PLATT
"Paralytic, "Verse Ten
Ariel

You say: The claw
Of the Magnolia,
Drunk on its own scents
Asks nothing of life.

I say: The flower
Is a seducing actress.
Even when there is aging
After a star performance,
It still wears heavy perfume
Like an old woman.

The claw is forever in rapture.
Even when heavy dark leaves
Curtain death, it waits.
Then, after winter snow,
It affairs anew
And fills its glass
Again and again.

RETURN TO WALES

Ah, Mother Wales, I am your child come home,
Again to walk those paths of bygone years,
And clasp ghost-hands of those in deepest sleep
Who speak in silent nights of dreamers still
Amid moonbeams and star-filled beckoning.

How could I once have thought a sweeter song
Or truer kisses lay in warmer love
Away from you across a stormy sea?
It was a wretched struggling demon sure
Who would have slain me had your call not come.

Why did I leave your always peaceful scenes,
Green valleys, guarded well by cherubins?
The coalpits' dreary darkness held great men
Who are forever resting now with you.

Your actor sons haunt yet with many words.
Your poet sons inspire my soul today
In early morning hours whispering
To offer joyful tears when night descends
In shrouds of clouds of hope and shinning light.

I will go gently into waiting night.
Ah, Mother Wales, I am your child come home.

WELSH MINER

Before daybreak,
down into the mine
to dark;
returning at night
to dark.

On Sunday,
Amazing Grace;
lifted-up voices in hymn sing,
receiving strength
to load the coal.
Amen.

Across the sea,
a homeland nestling
close to motherbreast;
where brothers pen
words of sorrow,
act out scenes of woe.
Down into the mine
in the morning
to dark;
returning at night
to dark.

Don't they know
here in the new land
of Pennsylvania
there is seeking for light
and yearning
for wings like eagles;
desire soaring
above
down into the mine.

continued

Whistles blow, counting time:
Go down, go up, hammer coal,
die, be buried
shoveling;
darkness covering.

Sunlight is only
for halos
of angels.

I WILL CRY IN AUGUST

When pressing heat in August

embraces tired flowers

that have been performing

since their premier in spring;

When late afternoons hang heavily

until twilight blankets cover,

but bring no comfort;

And when clouds cover the moon,

stars struggle to shine;

When summer is dying,

I will cry --

I will cry in August.

FAIR FINALE

Cotton candy sweeps the air

like pink fragmented clouds.

Appealing luster is lost

when candied apples, partly devoured,

hit the ground.

The Ferris wheel no longer

cradles lovers.

The merry-go round has ceased

playing its happy tune

and the tents have been folded.

From somewhere out of the darkness

comes a haunting sound--

Just like at the opera

the fat lady is singing.

The fair is over.

WINTER PRELUDE

The Artist
paints in breathtaking hues . . .
An unseen breeze
travels briskly.
Blue skies deepen,
playing hide and seek
with the sun.
Leaves wave goodbye
to pumpkins,
And busy squirrels
prepare for winter.
Nostalgia fills the air
as memories flare
like dancing flames.
Evening stars shine
through ebon darkness
and crickets sing
autumn's final chorus.

The tea is hot
and warms the soul
before the freeze
and cold, cold bones.

PRELUDE TO THE NURSING HOME

Mrs. Merriweather,
leaning heavily on her cane,
walks slowly along the path
leading to the soft green grass
of the front lawn.

Bending down,
she lifts the sign
that fell in last night's wind,
and stabs the earth
again and again
with the word - SOLD

THE BRACELET

was in the hospital gift shop
almost four weeks;
Burnished, appearing pure gold.
She would ask to lift it out
to see it - too expensive for her.
Almost identical, Bob gave her one
many years ago: Clasp at the back,
two curved sides that fit
around the wrist.
When her college granddaughter,
Lisa, graduated she gave it --

Today a large white tag
is tied to the bracelet.
Marked down - $4.00.
In disbelief -- she says,
I'll take it. Beaming,
she slips it around
her wrinkled wrist.

Jenny, you can take me back
now. The wheelchair is rolled
down the hall to chemotherapy.

She waits. Looks at the
gold bracelet, touches it,
thinks it is beautiful
and a perfect fit.

AN AGING ACTRESS PREPARES
FOR HER OSCAR-WINNING ROLE

Ah, memories must you bring back flashes

Of treasured bygone years that once did glow?

And when the dreams of youth weren't cold ashes

And hopes not buried deep by winter's snow.

This fleeting tired old heart does not yearn now

For long-spent joys that will not come again;

A rendezvous is nearing -- my last bow --

To fade -- become an echo on the wind.

A silent stage I leave, the curtain down,

To face another realm, a special light,

And reaching up, I'll grasp a better crown

And star bright, sparkle, sparkle in the night.

There is no desire to begin anew

As my Director prepares the adieu.

TWILIGHT WALTZING

What does one do when they know
clouds will soon hide the sun,
that a dark curtain will cover
the light of the moon
and summer roses will not trail
the garden fence?

What does one do when they know
the dazzling leaves of Autumn
will fade too soon
and time will become cold?

When one knows the results
of a physical exam,
What do they do,
Oh, what do they do?

They dance as long as they can.

THE WAR TO END ALL WARS

There are no distant drums
beating.
The strife is here
on this battlefield
now.

A shaking heart is protected
inside a foxhole of stark white
hospital walls.
The only ammunition
flows through tubes.

After this conflict with Death
there will be an unknown terrain.
No cannon will roar.
No sound.

No drums
now.

The
Good
Earth

Robert W. Bennett

NOTHING WITHOUT LABOUR ©

About the Author

ROBERT W. BENNETT, born in 1928 in Albion, Michigan, started writing poetry at age 14. After serving two years of military service during the Korean War, he earned a BA from *Bob Jones University* and an MA from *Western Michigan University.*

Robert taught 6th grade, junior high English, senior high English and Spanish. He also taught in a one room country school; grades K-8. He owned and operated a day care center for children, and has worked as a counsellor in three rescue missions: *Wayside Cross Rescue Mission,* Aurora, IL, *Pacific Garden Mission,* Chicago, IL, and *Haven of Rest Rescue Mission,* Battle Creek, MI.

He is editor and publisher of **RB'S POETS' VIEWPOINT,** and he has written a book of poems for children. His poetry has been published in many small presses including: Poetic Page, Poets of Now, and Peninsula Poets.

Robert married Christine Parkhurst in 1959; they have four children and live in Battle Creek, Michigan

CONTENTS

YELLOW CANARIES _____ 2
THE GREAT GAME _____ 2
THEY FOUGHT FOR FREEDOM _____ 3
THE WAR HORSE _____ 4
TO REMEMBER AND TO HONOR _____ 5
OH, COMRADES! _____ 6
AFTER THE GREAT TRANSACTION _____ 6
THE BABE OF GLORY _____ 7
HE HAD A PLAN _____ 8
THE GULLS AND THE WIND ARE ONE _____ 8
COLD CONQUEROR _____ 9
THE GOOD EARTH _____ 10
RIVER TRIP AT TWILIGHT _____ 11
SONNET XX _____ 12
SONNET XIV _____ 12
SONNET XII _____ 13
THE ICY TOMBS _____ 14
HIS FREEDOM _____ 15
AN OLD WOMAN BENT OVER _____ 16
THE GREAT DECLINE _____ 17
THE BEE IS IN THE CLOVER _____ 18
SIX GOOD MEN _____ 18
BIG GAME _____ 19
THE IMPECCABLE MR. HICKERSON _____ 20
BONE OF MY BONE _____ 20
A GLIMMER OF HOPE _____ 21
THE WALL CAME DOWN _____ 22
I WALKED ON HALLOWED GROUND _____ 23
A NEWBORN'S VIEW _____ 24

YELLOW CANARIES

The yellow canaries that sing in the sunshine
are harbingers of good times coming.
The patio warms after late breakfast.
Marla is busily employed in starched
white. The sun climbs in the sky;
the clouds arrange themselves in pictures
we try to describe: this is the mountain
we saw in Africa: that is the bullfighter
in Spain. The lawn beckons, the stream
and the gulf. It's time for another safari.

THE GREAT GAME

The man alone still as death
ponders square by square
the geometric pattern there where
jostled king fights for breath

while stubborn rook holds the fort
and wanton queen roams wild
the board with bishop mild
and pawn pricks Pegasus to cavort.

THEY FOUGHT FOR FREEDOM

Colonel Robert Shaw
trained his men with care.
They looked at him in awe.
They saw a white man dare
to set aside riches
and his place in society
to lead them in a bloody fight,
to give them freedom and the right
to be men.

Before the battle they had prayers;
the night illumined by the flares
of bombardments grim.
They closed with a hymn.
"The Lord is by our side," said
one of them.
Another said, "We are men."

The battle was fierce;
the odds were great.
They saw a bullet pierce
their commander. His fate
was sealed with their own.
This white colonel was thrown
into the mass grave
of men no longer slaves.

THE WAR HORSE

I am astride the war horse
that climbs the dark mountain.
Out comes the great force
from the Eternal Fountain.
Out comes the calibre of men
showing desperation in their eyes,
knowing they'll not come again,
grasping the mists of the gray skies.
The Death-Scythe is diligent;
the hills, mottled with stains,
are mellowed, yellowed and intransigent.
The time clock that pertains
to ravages of war clicks
methodically on. Nothing remains
of the old life, a few tricks
with a handkerchief shaken,
a few crumbs from a dinner partaken.
Mourn for me after my decease.
Make revel for me after my release.

TO REMEMBER AND TO HONOR

We gather here on the ground fallow.
We surely know the efforts to hallow
are vain. The bodies have enriched this ground;
the spirits have enshrined this ground.
Able-bodied men women are one with the earth.
They have given the frightful place a new birth.
We shall not know the terror that persuaded,
nor shall we grip the horror that pervaded
every hill and glen. But we know the place we revere.
We come together; we gather here
to solemnize, to remember and to honor
the ones we knew and loved. We ponder
on the sacrifice, on the great and proud position
of the men and women and their great propitiation.

OH, COMRADES!

Oh comrades, how many of us
went down to the courthouse, got on the bus
that took us away from our friends,
our parents, our town where nothing ends
but goes on forever in memory's arena.
How many of us stayed in the green
fields of foreign lands never to return,
never to mingle, never to burn
steaks at the fourth of July picnic.
The light-hearted jesting as the picked
left for war. The solemn tones,
the tears, as we return to the stones
of our home town. A tear for the comrade
in arms, a place in the heart that's sad.
It was a light thing-- going to war.
It was heavy coming home, sober and heart-sore.

AFTER THE GREAT TRANSACTION

The Transeptal arms reach
to all the earth.
The Transcribed Word shall teach
from lowly birth
before the Triumph, after the Triumph,
after the great Transaction.
Bear the news; greet the Holy One
in the early morn.
Shepherds greet Him
in the manger born.
Women are in the garden,
angels near the tomb,
men gather in the upper room.
Victory over death is celebrated.

THE BABE OF GLORY

A carpenter and his wife
were on a long journey;
they were expecting a new life.
The inns were all full
and Mary was weary.
They found a resting place
in a lowly stable
this holiest of nights.
Mary and Joseph received grace
from the Father of lights.
The shepherds saw the angels
and heard the glad story.
They left their sheep and came
to see the Babe of Glory.
The star shone down
on the sleepy little town,
and wise men traveled far
to worship the newborn king.
The animals in the stable
looked on in silent joy,
and Mary rejoiced to see God's Son,
and Mary hugged her little boy,
and said, "He is King, Thy will be done."

HE HAD A PLAN

the deep measureless love of God for man
He searched him out He had a plan
when in the garden He Said, "Where are you?"
He had a plan He followed through
with robes of skin he clothed them
and letters of love He wrote them
the rich earth He gave them to till
their destiny on earth to fulfill
though they were shaken by their fall
they had a Rescuer stand tall
before time began He had a plan
He'd send His Son to rescue man

THE GULLS AND THE WIND ARE ONE

the gulls and the wind are one
their passage alike under the sun
when the wind is still
the gulls fly quiet and will
from time to time
in their flight sublime
swoop for a morsel of food
but when the wind has wooed
them with a blast severe
they wing their way to veer
between the rock and the tree
and swift and sure and free
they are the visual part
of the wind's soul and heart

COLD CONQUEROR

Tall black sentinels stand across the lake,
Mute testimonies that autumn's hand
Has come, and having come, has made to break
The fragile clasp of summer's sunny band.

The cold, gray water rippled in waves,
Swept by the cutting western wind,
Laps against deserted docks and laves
Sunken stones against deep bottom pinned.

Chameleon earth cocks its weather eye
And changes from green garb into brown.
Distant stars are brighter, colder in the sky:
Lifeless leaves sail into the waves and drown.

The bright, gay world is gone and is replaced
By a weary one and wan, which settles down in pain
And dead defeat to endure grim-faced
The rigor-mortis grip of winter's reign.

THE GOOD EARTH

He remembers the redolent
earth after spring plowing;
the pungent smell
of the earth
during a summer shower;
the earth holds him
and possesses his being
in a maternal way
as he has not entirely
become separate from
his mother- she still
has her influence-
and so the earth,
large and nutrient-filled,
ever instills in his being
the warmness and welcome
from an energy-giver
and the sense of rightness
and comfort
from a supplier of strength.

RIVER TRIP AT TWILIGHT

River's down this year.
Grass is growing on the sand bars.
Herons fly near
the white house where the cars
are parked in rows.

Fish are jumping in the twilight
while the river flows
on down and ripples widen
to envelope our canoe.

Paddles dip and flash.
Raucous cries of crows
accompany the splash
of turtles going under.
We turn around and head
for home as the thunder
portends a wet night, but dry bed.

SONNET XX

This schism we have seen before,
have seen its most blatant form in war.
Recriminations come swiftly,
as we have seen in past relationships.
The language of the heart has no quips
to waste on transitory meetings
in the night. Carry her back to me
on the wind; carry her back to me
with breathless speed. The ever-
moving eyes see all. The cumbersome clouds
hover-- a pall of smoke obscures sight.
From sophistry's house there is a mockery
of human rights and justices;
from sophistry's tongue a lapping up of truth.

SONNET XXIV

I search the heavens with pensive gaze
the magnitude of space when I'm alone
the multitude of stars many questions raise
God's handiwork displayed while on His throne
He holds the universe in quantum space
and nothing falters in the great design
every atom exquisitely in place
consummate artistry and wealth combine
to make a universe of proportion vast
in which man is but a speck of dust
he displays now as in the past
a massive urge to satisfy his wanderlust
undaunted he climbs the interstellar stair
and makes new discoveries with flair

SONNET XXII

By the hearth, by the fireside I watch
the flames swirling in the air.. They flow
toward the oracle of humanity's folly.
The sparks that they engender form
myriad, sparkling, temporary ghosts.
They are the hosts of smoke-filled rooms;
they tell the tales of bone-filled tombs.
The eerie embers of the after-glow
expound on the gravity of life
beyond the grave and hold forth for hours
on pain's easement, and no more strife
for earth's huddled masses, no more powers
that be, no more flatulent futility.
Ashes that fall from the grate show life's brevity.

the icy tombs

the frozen wastes are empty now;
many carcasses are lying still--
inarticulate. many skulls on the brow
looking out upon the valley and the hill,
speaking voiceless words that drift
on howling winds across the icy plains,
making mockery of life, do not lift
a shred of hope, but banish brains
to icy tombs. fleshless limbs brandish
silent signals in the snow and crash
the barrier of bones, sending outlandish
messages to ghostly membranes of ash.
the hills echo the chilling sound.
the bones are rigid in the frozen ground.

HIS FREEDOM

His freedom was in the open spaces;
it was not in his nature to die
in a noisy crowded nursing home.
The closing in of four walls and choking
encumbrance of life extending machines
were to be avoided by any means.
He must search for the old freedom back
in the old village where the spirits
gather in the autumn days of council.
His blanket and a flickering fire were
his only comfort in the long night vigil.
He found his freedom in mid-afternoon:
a lone hawk soared in the azure sky.

AN OLD WOMAN BENT OVER

An old woman bent over,
picked up a bottle and slipped it
into her bag. The weight of years
kept her bent; the lines on her face
lent credence to the theory she
had seen hard times. Where
are the children, the husband,
the pretty cottage in the suburb?
Where is the joy of living,
the inscrutable blood lines flowing,
the glowing inner peace? All gone.
Nothing remains but the tremulous gait,
the gnarled fingers that once caressed
loving children, the matted tresses,
once a beautiful halo. There she goes,
a bag of bones with memories faded
as an old photograph.

THE GREAT DECLINE

The garbled, gray fog of age creeps
down the unraveled edge of the brain.
The slinking sloth of time leaps
the chasm of yesteryear and cranes
its neck to see the ravaged inner ear.
The coincidental chimera of chills
is awash in the sinus and the eyes blear.
The dread demon of ague our being fills.
What steady gait can we muster?
What clear-eyed gaze can we bring forth?
Can we bring back the skin's luster
of forgotten youth? Can we cavort
in jaunty dance with nimble retinue
of thought? What parsimonious hold
do we have on reality, and can we imbue
our life with actions brave and bold?

THE BEE IS IN THE CLOVER

The bee is in the clover now.
The wind is in the trees.
The leaves are full of chlorophyll
and rippling in the breeze.
The butterflies flit by in full color. Will
you be present at the metamorphosis?
The boys and girls are playing in the field.
They are close-- on the precipice
of puberty. The bee is done. The yield
is sweet. The leaves are fallen on the ground.
The butterflies have changed to worms.
The boys and girls are over the edge; their voices sound
different. The pattern of their play has new forms.

SIX GOOD MEN

What have the years brought us in retrospect?
  They have brought us very close I expect.
Can you imagine what I'd look like in white?
  You'd look great in anything tonight.
Have you noticed that the neighbors are all here?
  We should have a barbecue-- it's the time of year.
Remember, you're so prone to burn the meat.
  I'm so prone I cannot move my feet.
Well, my dear, are you ready for that trip?
  Well, my dear, I'm afraid I've lost my grip.
  I can't begin to tell you how this feels.
Love, you've got six good men instead of wheels.

BIG GAME

Rambling down rhythmical junctures,
the leopards make mythical punctures,
closeted in copse, masking their noise,
the cats wait for their prey.   The boys
scatter in front banging on pans;
we follow with rifles waiting the chance
to bag big game.
The sun bears down; the dust is choking.
The sweat rolls down; the rifles are smoking.
The boys retreat with angular tread;
they run back with anxious dread.
We press on without caution.
We want results, we want action,
we want big game.
There is sudden confrontation.
The cats have their daily ration:
we are the big game!

THE IMPECCABLE MR. HICKERSON

The impeccable Mr. Hickerson
lived in a world detached
with his books and his cats.
When he sat down to a succulent dinner
he was above mundane contingencies.
His sophisticated manner was never brunted
by the common, everyday trifles;
any interruptions were always shunted
to one side.
He never bothered to hide
his feelings of disdain
for the gardener's circumlocutions.

When the wind brought his house down
and the neighbors were fleeing,
he went right on being
the impeccable, imperturbable Mr. Hickerson.

BONE OF MY BONE

From Adam's rib she came
a solitary, significant dame.
She came to Adam help to give.
He was delighted to see her live.
He doted on this winsome gal
and noted in his diary, "She's a pal.
If ever we leave this garden of charm,
this wonderful doll will be on my arm."

A GLIMMER OF HOPE

In all the crassness of assembly line living
there is a pocket here and there of glimmering
self-respectability. Birds fly in the park.
Children die after dark in stinking tenements.
Discolored streets hem in stacked-up homes,
and broken street lamps fail to illumine
patches of weeds in vacant lots. But in several
windows we see star-gazers, and at dawn
a few joggers with new sweat bands dodging
refuse trucks. A mother scrubs a few worn out
clothes for kids stifled in baking inner city,
and a teacher, weary of lethargy,
looks inside a dreamer's heart and takes pity.

THE WALL CAME DOWN

The wall came down
tell it around the town
long years after the war
the wall exists no more
how long did it take to fall?
too long when measured by
lost lives and anguished hearts
but time passed
the people's desire
for freedom grew silently
in their breast
we all know the rest
they gathered in the street
they began to repeat
the wall must come down
the wall must come down
and the leaders relented
and the people vented
their pent up emotions
on the wall
they attacked it
with fingers and knives and hammers
they danced on it
they embraced loved ones
they embraced strangers
their long confinement was over
the wall was not strong enough
to withstand freedom's charge
yes the wall came down
thank God the wall came down

I WALKED ON HALLOWED GROUND

I walked on hallowed ground today
the ivory towers in grand display
the fathers of our country
stand in monuments of liberty
their words engraved in stone and hearts
enthrall us and the echo starts
a warm refrain of national pride
that swells to sea and mountainside
and reverberates around the world
the lofty sentiments -- the flag unfurled

A NEWBORN'S VIEW

Sent out by rocket's mighty blast
to view the earth from outer space,
held by umbilical tether,
to see as newborn earth's panorama,
the continents outlined in stark contrast
with the oceans blue,
to realize that earth's peoples
are one human race,
not separated as in the past.
If every human being could see
this newborn's view
and treat his brother with familial regard
and know that all people have a common bond
from creation to the final trumpet sound.

Transformation

By Kathleen Lee Mendel

About the Author

KATHLEEN LEE MENDEL was born in Bay City, Michigan. Her husband, James, is employed by a major electrical construction firm, and they travel extensively throughout the United States. One of her daily affirmations is, "I move with ease through time and space." Her daughters, Candy and Cindy, live in Michigan. One of the drawbacks to a life in constant motion is the time not spent with her grandson, Ryan, whom she adores.

She is the past-editor and founder of *Telstar Publishing*. Kathleen is currently studying Ancient Egypt and the Myth and Lore of the American Indians. She is working on a series of poetry books based on her studies. A few of the Egyptian pieces have already been published and are included in this collection.

Kathleen is an avid reader and has been writing since childhood. She retired from Corporate America in 1988 and now spends all her available time writing novels, short stories, columns and poetry. She writes a Poetry Market Column for *Recording and Publishing News,* a Book Review Column for *The Writers Companion* and has also written newspaper articles and a Business Etiquette Column that appeared in four monthly publications. She has won or placed in a multitude of national and international poetry contests and has accumulated hundreds of publishing credits.

Kathleen is an accomplished photographer and has won several photography awards. Her work was purchased by *Freedom Greeting Cards* and distributed throughout the country. In 1990 her photography was on display near Cincinnati, Ohio in her "first" one-woman show.

She belongs to several poetry organizations and is a member of the board of directors for the *Southern Poetry Association*. Kathleen is a graduate of *The Institute of Children's Literature* and has several non-related degrees. Her first children's novel, **General Chew-Waggle,** will be released in 1992.

Credit acknowledgement and a warm "thank you" to the editors of; *Cer*Ber*Us, Canto, Cosmic Trend, Dear Magnolia, Hemispheres, Kaleidoscope, Lucidity, Minnesota Ink, Recording and Publishing News, Puck N Pluck, Parnassus, Poetic Page, The Muse, The Poetry Peddler, The Poets Newsletter, and Verve.*

CONTENTS

APPROACHING THE CITY _____ 2
SIDEWALK SALE _____ 3
BUS STOP 9 _____ 3
ORPHAN TRAIN _____ 4
BASKETBALL IN THE PARK _____ 5
BACKYARD COMBAT ZONE _____ 6
SOJOURN INTO WOMANHOOD _____ 6
LIVING COVENANT _____ 7
SHATTERED _____ 8
CAGED EXISTENCE _____ 8
TRASH _____ 9
MORNING COFFEE _____ 9
SEEDS _____ 10
SOJOURN _____ 10
SENTINEL MAN _____ 11
HER LAND _____ 12
UNNOTICED _____ 13
TIME _____ 13
WINGS OF STONE _____ 13
TRANSFORMATION _____ 14
THE GARDEN, BETWEEN _____ 14
RAIN, SLEET, SNOW _____ 15
DRIFT WOOD _____ 15
RAINBOWS _____ 15
WINTER HANDOUT _____ 16
GULL MORNING _____ 16
CAGED DEATH _____ 16
CHEETAH _____ 17
RED FOX SCAVENGER _____ 17
RELATIVITY _____ 18
HOSTAGE EXECUTION _____ 19
AMOROUS MOON _____ 20
BAK'S FAREWELL TO NEFERTITI _____ 21
THE NAMING AT THE HOUSE OF LIFE _____ 22
AWAKING INTO AWARENESS _____ 23
THE CYCLE OF LIFE _____ 24

APPROACHING THE CITY

A five hour cat-purr
from my car engine
had deafened my ears.
With strained eyes,
I watched
the horizon end at the lip
of a sprawling valley;
in the distance,
a dark-bottom cloud carpet
laid like a dirty crib blanket
over an irregular cluster
of towering
steel-glass structures.
Descending toward
the flat-bed city,
I watched
salt-white cloud columns
erupt
from rusted steel-stacks
and dissolve into the crib blanket
that blocked their escape.
Nausea griped me
as I glanced toward
the highway shoulder
and read,
   "Welcome to Cleveland."

SIDEWALK SALE

She leans against the street light
while neon signs flash
a rainbow of color
across her tight sweater.

A long black Cadillac
pulls to the curb;
she trashes her cigarette,
sways catlike,
and advances
toward her next paycheck.

BUS STOP 9

Glass pyramids pierce the twilight
as a thread-bare child,
deep in his private darkness,
gropes toward Bus Stop 9,
and the familiar cat-purr
of the idling diesel engine.

Sudden screaming tires
of a delivery truck
pull him to quick death.
The people pause,
momentarily, before
continuing their pilgrimage
along the merchants pavement.

ORPHAN TRAIN

Tons of machined steel,
powered by hand-fed-coal,
labors to pull its nomadic cargo
through clusters of dense fog.

Within its attached cages,
the eyes
of abandoned children
stare through glass openings
straining to identify
illusive, passing shadows
while silently listening
to the rickety-clack
of the vibrating
rusty-iron-rails.

An unseasonal fog
hangs like a damp flour sack
around the foot worn platform.
Farmers,
with leather like skin,
discuss the coming harvest
while waiting
to pick
green fieldhands.

BASKETBALL IN THE PARK

A boy, not yet ten -
tries hard to understand
why his father
farms barren land.

He has hens to feed
and cows to milk
but he stops for a moment
to pet a gray-black kitten -
softer than silk.

Late into the night,
he reads by candlelight
about places far away
where children are allowed to play
while he must work,
  harvesting tons of hay.

In dreams,
he meets new friends;
playing basketball
in a city park.

The morning light
clears his head -
he jumps out of bed.
Tired muscles
greet a new dawn;
within moments,
his private dreams
  are gone.

BACKYARD COMBAT ZONE

Perched
on a weathered stockade fence,
the sentinel-crow
watches
the stone-throwing children
pause
       to select
              their weapons.
Armed,
they continue to maneuver
the wooded terrain;
the crow's piercing squawk
halts their approach:

       The cloudless sky fills
       with hundreds
       of fluttering black wings
       that drive
       the child-commandos
       back
       to their brick-patio
       safety zone.

SOJOURN INTO WOMANHOOD

(for my daughter, Candy)

Another decade
seals itself
inside the wooden picture frames
randomly arranged
across my plastered walls;

As I stared at your photograph
memory fragments escaped
into the darkened room
and for a few brief moments
I relived
the life decisions
that shattered our girl scout images;
you erected scaffolding and leaped
youth walls into womanhood
while I sought freedom
from materialistic existence;
many times
our sojourn changed
but in all moments
we were one.

LIVING COVENANT
"Poets must reject the past, and embrace
instead the unglamorous domestic realities
of the age." *- ELIZABETH BARRETT BROWNING -*

Crouched on the frayed sofa
she bites her fingernails
and waits
like a hunting house cat
ready to pounce;
As he enters the room
her jagged, raw nerves
explode
and she screams...
demanding his share of the rent.
He pushes her aside,
grabs a cold beer,
and attempts to mentally erase
her presence,
until his desire
remembers
their arrangement.

SHATTERED

I gazed at the flickering candles
casting elusive shadows across
the title-lined-walls of our library;
soft, classical music
eased my anguished spirit
and slowly wrapped phantom bandages
around my yearning heart.
A distant phone rang and rang
as I methodically searched
desk drawers for glue,
as if life were a china tea pot
that could be mended.

CAGED EXISTENCE

(For my grandson, Ryan)

Tears trickle down
his stained cheeks
as his tot-like hands lower
the shoe-box-coffin
into the fresh dug earth;
He shoves a popsicle-stick-cross
to mark the tulip-bed-grave,
mumbles, "Now I lay
wild bird down to sleep,"
covers the hallowed spot,
and hurries
toward the hanging wire-compound
to feed the new,
store bought,
green-and-yellow chirpper.

TRASH

The girl,
clutching a plastic bag,
inches her way along
the deep shadow void
cast by looming buildings,
and scurries toward
a rusty trash dumpster.

Quickly,
she lifts the heavy cover,
deposits her bloody bundle,
and aborts her soul.

MORNING COFFEE

Sunlight penetrates
the still darkness
as I wake
to an empty house,
and stand, bare,
like a soldier
out of uniform.

I make coffee,
pouring two cups,
slowly sipping mine
while yours chills
to the silence
of terminated love.

SEEDS

We sipped time's vintage wine
in soft candle light,
loving each other
through cold winter nights.
Wakening from a lovers sleep,
we touched the blossoms of spring.
Walking the beach in summer
we exchanged golden rings.
We watched glorious fall leaves
race toward the ground -
And, in memory's debris,
      our love seeds can be found.

SOJOURN

Caught within
the magic circle
with future beckoning:
    we meet.

Awakening danger
of unlimited knowledge
or miracle wisdom:
    sojourn begins.

Morning brightness
showing direction
with guidance growing:
    we start.

Corrected direction
reflecting autumn
and chilling winter:
    sojourn ends.

SENTINEL MAN

Old eyes scan unfurrowed fields
as he pictures
a once prosperous farm.
His cup was long filled
with life's bittersweet wine;
wife buried in family plot;
sons gone to mine city gold,
rotted squash hulls
marking the last crop.

He looks to the sky
from long habit,
crushes a handful
of black warm earth,
and turns, slowly,
toward an empty home
and a barren life.

HER LAND

She raises her hand,
blocking the noon day sun.
Her grandchildren play,
laughing happily as they run.

Gazing across her rippling corn
ready to crest,
she recalls the day
she migrated west,
and, how her gentile family
survived the wilderness.

Alone, detached
from the society of man,
she and her husband
worked the virgin land.
Chilled, from a haunting image
of him in his prime,
she wonders if they'll meet,
again, somewhere in time.

Her youngest son,
new bride at his side,
kisses her cheek,
coaxing her out for a ride.
He heads his Jeep
toward the high land to the east.

At the top of the knoll,
her thoughts run deep.
Contented,
far from the cities of fear and crime,
she whispers to the wind,
       "This land is mine."

UNNOTICED

I am blank paper
kept in the back
of your black leather
address book.

TIME

I stare at my watch,
pondering the fragile sentinels
who march from number to number:
  seconds to minutes;
  minutes to hours;
  and days to years.
I envision their ultimate
advance toward eternity,
and quickly rip
the albatross from my wrist.

WINGS OF STONE

The Phoenix of old
flew high and bold,
and to all who saw
brought gifts of gold.
The phoenix today
is far away
with wings of stone
and feet of clay.

TRANSFORMATION

On the hillside, a lean fox
Sniffs the crisp autumn breeze.
Spooked by an eerie whistling,
He vanishes through leaf-barren trees;

A gray squirrel scampers,
Gathering winter food,
Anticipating Mother Nature's
Forthcoming mood.

A monarch's velvet shadow
Passes wildflowers, withered brown.
The forest inhabitants brace
For snow to cover the ground.

Dry skeletal cattails sway
Like a bronze wind-chime,
And the transforming season
Signals the passage of time.

THE GARDEN, BETWEEN

Dancing crystals cling within the
forgotten space,
welcoming an untouched rock, snared
by the tangled maze.
Splashes of sunlight skip,
carelessly, atop withered vines
of untamed wine.
Cloud-like-clusters of frozen
white-water, melt, feeding
the hungry soil.
Shadows leap the blue-gray points
that hold tight the dense plot.
Mold-encased chunks of redwood
struggle for freedom.
Foliage skeletons, guarded by piercing
worriers, silently labor.
Twigs, unattached, in scattered
disarray, watch dark gray shadows
fondle rusted statues.
Citizens of the habitat, undisturbed,

RAIN, SLEET, SNOW

R ain changed to sleet and invaded the late
A utumn woodland, as
I observed the squirrels preparing their
N ests to ensure their continuance;

S ummer warmth had succumbed to
L ow temperature nights that tested their
E ndurance. Leafless branches signaled an
E arlier frost had penetrated their skyway,
T erminating green life till spring.

S earching diligently for
N eeded nutrition, they remained
O blivious to my presences, and hurried to
W interize their environment.

DRIFT WOOD

I found it washed upon the shore -
this bleached skeleton of some gone tree,
its nose ignominiously buried
in the hot sand.
I dug it out and dragged it home
to place it in my garden:
          this white bone of a ship,
          its prow always seaward,
          its stern well anchored
between pansies, petunias,
and pearl pink conch shells
from an ocean far away.

RAINBOWS

R adiant beams of colored light
A nchor themselves to a skycanvas;
I lluminating a cleansed horizon -- creating a
N atural phenomenon that is envied
B y brushsmiths who have spent their lifetime
O bserving this priceless masterpiece,
W ondering how they can duplicate and
S ell what nature freely creates.

WINTER HANDOUT

A bright cardinal
perches
on a leafless branch
near a snow-covered feeder
like a Salvation Army Santa
waiting for
his bread-crumb children.

GULL MORNING

Hungry sea gulls
battle for the tide's bounty
while laughing children
grab the empty shell-houses
to decorate their city lives.

CAGED DEATH

At incandescent daybreak, the sun
warms my shivering hands
as I watch a weathered-caretaker
feed a mangy, growling lion.

Sensing the lions imminent death,
I focus my camera
on his scarred face,
and his eyes pierce mine
          with his immured terror.

CHEETAH

The hunting Cheetah, with spotted yellow fur,
sneaks like a commando toward her prey.
The grazing antelope sees only a blur
before its blood is spilled in the heat of day.
Four Cheetah children wait in a hidden den
to eat the kill while mother guards the door,
and when the food is gone, she'll hunt again;
her mothering becomes a constant chore.
She teaches hunting lessons every day
to help her young survive natures law,
and if a curious kitten, in its play,
falls victim to a predatory claw,
        she gazes for a moment, steeped in pain,
        then turns to tend the children who remain.

RED FOX SCAVENGER

Alert, his cold paws ramble
an eon old lava bed
that crawls across
the widespread basin
like a patchwork quilt;

He pauses, ears erect,
and gazes into the farness
toward dark bottom storm clouds
that obscure Grand Teton peaks.

His breath mists the frigid air
as he sniffs
the snow blanketed
harvest residue
shimmering in icylace.

Cautiously, he edges toward
a rectangular cottonwood enclosure
and human scent.

RELATIVITY

(For Richard Bach)

Outside my cabin,
the woodland resembled
a crystalline sphere.
As I stoked the fire,
I thanked the cosmos
for being transferred here;
The top of my mountain
was posted, private-land
and I felt detached
from the chaos of man.
Winter's wind
was a howling -- growling rage
as I prepared to enter
a higher stage;
He circled my chair,
ready for his nap,
then Schroedinger's cat
jumped onto my lap.
I sensed he wondered
when we'd depart
as I felt the quickening
pace of his heart.
I listened to his rumbling,
low and deep,
as my astral companion,
snored, fast asleep.
Tossing Planks' book aside,
I knew he was dreaming
about ruling his pride.
Relaxed, my eyes slowly closed--
I reach alpha by visualizing
a pure, red rose;
Like the lion and the lamb
in shared sleep,
Our souls energized
        for a quantum leap.

HOSTAGE EXECUTION
(September 1918, Moscow - Russia)

Outside my barred window,
the frigid wind whistles
through the leaf barren courtyard;
I huddle against the mold encrusted
damp, stone cell wall.
I cover my ears but I cannot escape
the Russian screams
that penetrate my wood-steel door.
I am quartered. Death's footsteps approach . . .
Dare I ask why, Nicholas?
Why your vision overlooked the Cheka?*
Peasants starved during winters chill
while you, the mighty czar, flaunted privilege!
Infected by power, you could not identify defeat
until the footfalls of the February Revolution
forced your dethroning.

Was little Alexis wearing his sailor fabric
when a Bolsheviks bullet penetrated his brain?
Was it a traitors-thread that Empress Alexandra
pulled through her imperial cross-stitch
as she listened to the quad-duchesses
beg for their plundered, unfulfilled lives?

When the blackcloth blanketed my vision
the wind whispered that you live.
Before death embraces me I must know,
Nicholas, does the wind lie?

*Cheka - a political police force that established
Communist rule by terror.

AMOROUS MOON

Armana Period;
Anken-Aten [The heretic Pharaoh]
The Great Royal Wife, Nefertiti
New Kingdom [1378 - 1362 B.C.]

Capricious moon, nocturnal traveler,
I raise my arms in joyous welcome
as you illuminate my private darkness;

Your knowingness watches me
embrace the "Beautiful One"
until her willfulness crumbles
and we become like cornflowers
tossed in a midday breeze.
I lift the stone-reeds
that cage her lapis lazuli heart
       and sow fertile seeds
              that will endure eternity...

BAK'S FAREWELL TO NEFERTITI
Armana Period:
Anken-Aten [The heretic Pharaoh]
The Great Royal Scalptuor, Bak
New Kingdom [1378 - 1362 B.C.]

My beloved, "Beautiful One",
who dwelt in the light of truth;
Through the eyes of a mortal worshipper,
one last time, I gaze at your golden body,
heavy with the trappings of death.
Your earthly features float in my mind,
riding moon-like above a firey horizon.

Sorrow swells in my heart
as I caress the divine hand
that once ruled the soul of the Two Lands.
I yearn to hear the enchantment
that once poured from your lips.
I pray our Unseen Creator
will rejuvenate your limbs
and in the boldness of midday light,
I will, once again, embrace my beloved.

My splendid, "Beautiful One",
so free and unceremonious,
call upon my name for ever and ever,
And I shall not fail you!
We are one, eternally....

THE NAMING AT THE HOUSE OF LIFE

Amarna Period: from the teachings of
Akhen-Aten [The heretic Pharaoh]
New Kingdom [1378 - 1362 B.C.]

I watch celestial bodies fade
into the coming forth of day.
Light pinpoints reach across the horizon
and chase nocturnal shadows from my cell.

I greet the days birth and joyously prepare
            for the naming.
I tremble in knowing
my blood is that of an unwashed scribe,
apprentice to the great Amenhotep.

Solemnly, I prepare red-blood-ink.
My reed pen splits its smooth surface
and I perceive Maats' feather
spiral toward the scale of hearts.
I am living in truth.

I contemplate the blue lotus
slowly opening to greet Ra
and inhale its tingling fragrance.
I catalogue Pharaoh's wheat-harvest
and name the priest of Aten
who will consume its vital fibers.

What I behold and mark
    shall be remembered,
        and that which is remembered,
            lives...

AWAKING INTO AWARENESS

From the Temple of Isis
at Philae; Reign of Ptolemy II
Philadelphus Period [285-246 B.C.]

I walk Philae's landline,
my sleep-heavy eyes open
transcending the stone pillows
of the dreamless;

I become the morning mist
    devoured by the rising sun.
I exist within the lotus blossom
    opening into light.
I merge with the circling falcon
    casting long shadows
        across desert sands.
I transcend the sandstone cliffs
    towering about the sparkling Nile.
I blend into the morning fire
    crackling in a summer breeze.

My cleansed eyes blink and
I move from unknowing into knowing;

I am a shaft of light,
    eternal and at peace.

Philae:
An island in the nile where the ancient Egyptian Temple
of Isis was located. The temple complex was moved to
the island of Agilkia when the new High Dam was built
at Aswan in 1971 A.D.

THE CYCLE OF LIFE

I feel inner cold.
Darkness lies about me
in my winter of reflection.

From deep within I sense
flashing images of my recent
spring, summer, and fall.

The inner radiance of that spring.
The torridness of that summer.
And, the changing glory of that fall.

My thoughts are taking form
as the light within grows brighter.

Once, again, I feel the promised
warmth and freshness
of a coming spring.

Again, I enter the cycle
          for lessons yet to learn.

Laurence W. Thomas

About the Author

LAURENCE W. THOMAS tried to prove that you <u>can</u> go home again. After a career of teaching in Uganda, Costa Rica, and Saudi Arabia, Michigan, and Florida, he returned to his home town of Ypsilanti, Michigan, and even to the house where his parents lived. He taught at Eastern Michigan University and Washtenaw Community College before retiring in 1992.

Overseas, Thomas combined the teaching of English with an interest in journalism. He did reviews for the *Uganda Argus* and was "culture editor" for the *Tico Times* in Costa Rica. While in Saudi Arabia, he sent a series of articles about his life there to a Michigan newspaper. During all this time, he continued his major interest in poetry which began when he won Hopwood awards in poetry and essay while taking a Master's degree at the University of Michigan. Upon resettling in Ypsilanti, Thomas collected his poems and published his first book, *Pursuits,* followed by five chapbooks of poetry. His poems and prose have appeared in *Peninsula Poets, Way Station, Sisyphus, Red Dancefloor, Bitterroot, Forms, The Wall Street Journal, Punch, Birders' World, Mr. Cogito, Oktoberfest, Blue Unicorn,* and several anthologies.

Thomas' interest in poetry has taken him to many workshops by such well-known writers as Jack Driscoll, David St. John, Edward Hirsch, Patricia Hooper, Janet Kaufman, Gary Gildner, Herb Scott, William Olsen, Alice Fulton, and William Stafford. Currently he is active in the Poetry Society of Michigan where he co-edited the 1990 anthology and edits their Newsletter. He <u>did</u> go home again but, of course, it wasn't the same home he left.

CONTENTS

GENESIS _____ 2

A GOOD YEAR FOR TULIPS _____ 3

THERE IS A GOD _____ 4

BODY AND SOUL _____ 5

TRIO FOR SOLO VOICE_____ 5

HAYDN'S SURPRISE SYMPHONY_____ 6

ETUDES _____ 7

COMMENCEMENT _____ 8

SHORE BIRDS _____ 9

ONE-LEGGED GULL _____ 10

SNAILS _____ 10

SATISFACTION _____ 11

LIFE CYCLE _____ 11

FRAILTY_____ 11

SENRYU _____ 11

TANKA _____ 11

FINAL VICTORY_____ 12

CITY AWAY_____ 13

WILDFIRE _____ 14

NOW AND THEN _____ 15

SIREN SONG _____ 16

THE LUCKY DRAGON _____ 17

WHAT CAN NEVER TOUCH ME _____ 18

HIDING PLACES _____ 19

FAME _____ 20

YOUR MOTHER WEARS
       GOLD LAMÉ COMBAT BOOTS _____ 21

REVIEW _____ 22

IMMORTALITY _____ 23

HOMING_____ 24

GENESIS

In the beginning it all seemed fairly clear
something rising out of something else and traceable
before inventors had something to write with
before science.

Evidence of adaptations from primordial origins
lost under layers of unclocked time on unnumbered pages
remain the unread story of growth and development
poorly preserved.

When explanations are in order
observers contrive theories to account for mysteries
gods for all things natural to make the supernatural
collectively acceptable.

Since language works with words for things
man became the only naming creature
ignorant that definitions of things not visible
lack accord:

dalmations are dogs and a dogwood a tree
but a god cannot be the same to two people
an invention by many unable to discern
natural explanations

ready to take advantage of those whose faith
blinds them from evidence and whose hopes
lie beyond the world of logical explanation
substance redefined.

Opinion succeeds when facts are incomplete
holds tenaciously after they are not to be denied
revered because it comes from ancient writ and
oral tradition.

continued

Believers without proof need reminding
with stars and crescent moons and crosses
with idols and relics and medals and prayers--
wishful thinking

and rewards are promised but rarely awarded
deferred because retribution is easier to administer
than recompense--healing more difficult
than death.

A GOOD YEAR FOR TULIPS

The neighbors walk their dogs or jog on by pretending.
I would do the same myself
look with terrified eyes on threatening buds
look away.

Faced down by his critics I can see
Van Gogh begging forgiveness.
Is what I do done for them
these markings never used to break new ground?

I must search for the blotch of blood on the sheets
raise the issue in my image without fearing condemnation.
During rehearsals Stravinsky throws up his hands
impatiently shouting play what you hear not what you see.

What I hear is my voice.
What I see no longer discourages
husbanded through hard seasons
untouched and innocent after the winter.

THERE IS A GOD

There is a God who does good things for you.
(How well Cordelia understood the value of nothing.)
I learned to lie at my mother's knee.
No word is wholesome to deceitful minds.

Can dissembling be sinful if not revealed?
They fault us who are not like them.
Prayers are answered when we change our minds.
I learned the lie at my mother's knee.

My father's weaknesses flow through me.
Is too much individualism bad for the soul?
Should I repeat what I did yesterday
When I learned lying at my mother's knee?

No word is deceitful to wholesome minds.
(How well Cordelia understood the value of nothing.)
Can dissembling be sinful if not revealed?
My father's weaknesses flow through me.

The formula that works repeatedly is science.
Is too much individualism good for the soul?
No word is wholesome to corrupted minds.
They fault us who are not like them.

Should I repeat what I did yesterday?
Their prayers are answered who change their minds.
Can dissembling be sinful if not revealed?
There is a God who does good things.

BODY AND SOUL

They looked for a man who would cry
for them on national television,
cry for the lost body of his son
after the flood, after the others
had been rescued or found in the debris,
a man who regretted the body
like sorrowing for a jewel
destroyed in the disposal.
The search would continue, he said.
If there is a soul, would it celebrate
what they might find?

TRIO FOR SOLO VOICE

I
am a dirigible
pushing
against the top of my hangar.
The gates are shut
and you are at your moorings
outside
loading for your voyage
                    or
I
am an anxious mother
watching her child leave.
I yell in warning
    "Don't play too hard"
    "Be careful!"
but you can't
    or don't
hear what I have to say
                    and
I cry out
from a dream
in pain
in doubt
in anguished fear
but you smile
and ask
    "Did you have a nice day?"
    "How are things?"

HAYDN'S SURPRISE SYMPHONY

We hated practicing. There were no
visions of recitals in concert halls
or just sitting idly at the piano
improvising. Music fails

forced in its creation or performance
into the limits of an hour
or reduced to childish arguments
about who would practice in the parlor.

But we knew the impishness of Haydn
how he contrived to keep his audience
awake with unexpected sudden
crashes in the strings and winds

so I feigned sleep while my sister played
that lulling melody Papa Haydn used.
My sister and I never tried
for harmony but as we amused

ourselves with crescendos and waking
each other up, we grew together finding
a closeness not from making
chords and dissonances but rather a blending

that families often never find. Our
little games were never played for other
people to enjoy but in that parlor
we were happy: just a sister and a brother.

ETUDES

The students groan
under the heavy burden of remembering Lear.
His tragic flaw, theirs.
Their fate, not quite the same:
they are not killed for sport
and having not yet committed adequate folly
they will keep their minds and daughters
but never gain what Lear almost gained
and Gloucester only temporarily lost.

        They write
        the answers coming
        from heads and pen
        and books they have not read
        and lectures not attended
        or slept through.

        They guess and write too much.
        What experience have they had
        of what the author thought?
        How equate the happenings
        in the book with those ideas
        which they have never had
        because no one ever told them?

A roomful of silence
like ceasing of bees
faces of vacancy
resplendent in newly-lost knowledge
as pens trace stains on paper
they strain.
               The brain
is predictable; knowledge is not.
Memories seldom fail
till put to the test--
when they are met with questions
never before encountered.
Round ruminant room
eyes wander to windows
(and sometimes to neighboring papers)
pursuing a clue to the truth--
passing answers.

COMMENCEMENT

Some leave lightly with sighs and whispers
leaving undisturbed that little balance
between the learner and the learned
and are seldom heard.

Others exit, tread heavy in the halls
echoing the message against the tilings of the mind
leaving nothing upset, upturned
between the learner and the learned.

Semesters end, begin again with resignation and relief.
Between, terminal attempts to gain
and simultaneously evade
with copied notes and incogitant aping

are weighed, inequitably assigned a grade
a compromise of what is earned
between the learner and the learned.
And the university doors lie gaping.

SHORE BIRDS

Early birds catch the warm of the sun
light on illusions to outpace reality
decked out to cover indulgences.
They scavenge edges of tides
ever ebbing beneath burning light
flirting with desuetude
seeking to gain what memories serve.
They claw their ways among accretions
smells of the dying, shells of the dead
under swelling rays as the sun
flies high over expectations.
They vie against gravity
matching accomplishments
competition stronger as the day grows old.

Heavily leaning on the horizon
as sagging sun slants resignation,
they harbor an emptiness
after their hard day's searching
and the last tide turns.

ONE-LEGGED GULL

Choose carefully the peopled places
the extremities of crowds

to stand out. We adapt
to our physiques

tutoring our actions in response
to how we are regarded.

The polished stone of my personality
reflects my youthful shyness

some of the facets still unbuffed
some of the edges rough and cutting.

I remember the self consciousness
of being skinny

picking flowers in left field
and learning the rhythms of classical music.

I know there is more to evolution than this
but if proof is needed here is a beginning.

SNAILS

Converging on sands flattened by routine
they emerge from their commonplaces and
wrapped in their egos against threatened rejection
their bravado against isolation
they wander or wade tides' slender margins
wrapped in their vanity avoiding detection.
Braving their ways in sea weeds and shells
they seek the acceptable, offer themselves
wrapped in their nudity against observation
naively fearing exposure.

SATISFACTION

a falling flower
meets its reflection lightly
touching the water

LIFE CYCLE

a butterfly poised
between the world of the worm
and oblivion

FRAILTY

ice encased branches--
crystal limbs of protection
so vulnerable

SENRYU

Chinese youth parade
through Tienanmen Square--
infants teasing a dragon

TANKA

The cat's ear flickers
as dreams of escaping prey
disturb its repose:
a chipmunk just out of
reach--

FINAL VICTORY

Events so affecting this city erupting are distant
in miles but not in spirit: This local team handing
final defeat to its season-long adversaries. Cele-
bration is in order; these celebrations lack just
that. Streets fill as the last ball whooshes through
its hoop; crowds gathered in bars and arenas to
watch large-screen televisions issue out like chil-
dren after school. Riverfront fireworks are gut-
tering candles compared to explosions in streets
burning, overturned automobiles. Whistling rock-
ets rising are a piccolo played pianissimo heard
against ambulances rushing to rescue those in-
jured, fire trucks wailing their ways toward fires.
Drums beating out victory rhythms are dim echoes.
In parades, television eulogies, speeches by dig-
nitaries, players, coaches, a voice is heard in one
of those inexplicable silent moments that some-
times come. "I wish you the joy of the worm," it says.

CITY AWAY

Arrival awakens this dawning city
aging away from passing the time
renewal gaining from ravage respected as
custom: tranquility balances yearning.

Discovery enriches this welcome city
escaping indifference to unwonted attentions;
meandering garden paths passing fountains
mix with tradition, beauty, utility.

Thought enlightens this sunset city
settling away from shocks and monotonies.
Clouds fold down over edges of mountains
before they dissolve to complete apprehension.

Comfort shelters this winter city
waiting warmly away from nonentity
gently enfolded in the palm of the mountain
surrounding, safe in its craggy enclosure.

WILDFIRE

I was to feel the heat for years
        after the ashes on the apple boughs cooled
        long after we no longer missed the grapes
a heat that lingered on my reddened face
guilt to liven family conversations
when our histories return to savage us.

It started in innocence
        the experimental quest for knowledge
        an elemental test of earth air water fire
while others were playing softball
in the backyard. We set our apparatus behind the barn
unaware that science fails in the hands of the inept.

We rushed unnoticed past the playing field
        to get brooms for beating at our guilt
        as we had seen fires put out before
but the orange of the flames reflected on our faces
gave us away even when we hid in the safety of the barn
where my sister discovered us playing an old Victrola.

The terror was punishment enough
        the threat to neighbors' houses
and firemen who came with stern faces.
There is no atonement for a blackened orchard and vineyard
like guilt and resolution never to repeat
what in the mind can never be extinguished.

NOW AND THEN

The snow is not so soft and deep and welcome.
I feel its threat crunching underfoot.
It is too much effort to put galoshes on.
I remember rushing out to make fairies in the snow.

The Santa Claus at Crowley-Milner's was real.
(Across the flat and the pastel snow two people go.)
It is too much effort to put galoshes on.
Roads are treacherous and I drive to work.

We fell asleep by chimneys and were carried off to bed.
All the pictures show us what we think we remember.
Could Vivaldi have known what snow is really like?
I feel its threatening crunch under my feet.

Snowball fights were all we knew of strife.
Could Vivaldi have known what snow is really like?
It was easy to find coal for my snowman's eyes.
Roads did not seem treacherous with my father driving.

All the pictures show us what we think we remember.
It was Christmas time at Hudson's and the Santa was real.
Almost any excuse will do to keep me home.
(Across the flat and the pastel snow two people go.)

I remember rushing out to make snow fairies.
We fell asleep by chimneys and were carried off to bed.
Snowball fights were all we knew of strife.
The snow is not so soft and deep and welcome.

SIREN SONG

When young Ulysses heard the sirens'
Treacherous singing, he had reason
To rejoice; courting danger, even wide awake
To jeopardy, rarely goes
Unpunished, but he was wont to sleep

In peril, and in horses, ending wars. Reason
Sits aloof from conflicts, puts to sleep
Offending causes and effects the silencing of sirens.
Accord is lost, leaving in its wake
Distrust, misunderstanding, when the envoy goes

Away because he is disinclined to reason
At the conference table. The U.N. sleeps
Its usefulness away and still the sirens
Sound their warnings, and innocents awake
To wonder how the battle goes.

Flashing lights, horns, bells, sirens
Alert those not involved to catastrophe, wake
Benighted senses to dilemma, give reason
To count blessings as the saying goes
And turn to restless, troubled sleep.

Prepared for, trouble often goes
Before it starts, giving way to reason
Through the safeguard of being awake.
Though they disobeyed him, his men were not asleep
When young Ulysses heard the sirens.

When sirens awake reason goes to sleep.

THE LUCKY DRAGON

The men of science turn the golden page.
The fishers leave to cultivate the sea.
Sing loud the coming of the peaceful age.

The Lucky Dragon clears the harbor to engage
In age-old harvest action; as they flee,
The men of science turn the golden page.

The other dragon roams the islands in a rage,
Lays eggs, so in their final hatching, we
Sing loud the coming of the peaceful age.

The Lucky Dragon's sailors disengage
Their engines off Bikini, do not see
The men of science turn the golden page.

The other dragon, restive in its cage,
Struggles, suddenly emerges, and is free.
Sing loud the coming of the peaceful age.

The meeting of the dragons sets the stage
Where scientists and fishermen agree.
The men of science turn the golden page;
Sing loud the coming of the peaceful age.

[The Japanese fishing boat, The Lucky Dragon,
was caught in the fallout of the atomic test on Bikini
and the fishermen were killed.]

WHAT CAN NEVER TOUCH ME

Things we can't explain
become religion:
water nymphs, the rainbow
all storms and disasters
the death of children and miracles
inventions to satisfy our gods
laying the blame somewhere else
so we never have to do anything.

        I called upon my soul one day
        but of course nobody was home.

Deities ultimately devolve
to what is good in my own eyes
sorting out beauty
an arbitrary decision that El Greco
is better than Watteau
Philip Glass than Puccini
strictures notwithstanding
we compare horses to oranges.

        The fruit of the tree in the midst of the garden
        makes a very good Waldorf salad.

My job--to deal when devils dance
undoing what can never touch me
a biblical monopoly on truth
the burning of the flag. No sensation
without sense makes me deaf
to the constant drumming on my door
pleas for money and teary causes
which already have their answers.

HIDING PLACES

Keep everything, you tell yourself
you will return someday to your books
your records your high school graduation picture
you don't need now and can't take with you.

Perhaps you will never open these boxes
stored away in the attic of your mind
or gathering memories in a basement--
treasures waiting for rediscovery.

Don't look back. Move from place to place
accumulating dying friendships, experiences
tailored to the moment, adding what you can
to shore up your defense against demands.

But the stash pulls at you like the tide
an evidence felt as the unreachable itch
that you are more than your parts, that memory
and recollection are what make up the soul.

FAME

Fifteen minutes fits fine, thank you.
We spend so much getting there
so much looking back and wallowing in it.

I acquire my knowledge piecemeal, forgetting
much along the way, depending on my books
going into the past to patch up the present.

Shakespeare probably had a phrase for it
or the Bible. I tap precedents for proof
experience for a philosophy

I can call my own, not needing
the Assumption of Mary, the big bang theory
as irrelevant to me.

Assuming that a seed will grow, the birds
will fly south for the winter
is enough though not everything, not

an answer when the cycle ends. After a game
is finished another will begin, another
day even after the darkest night.

If it happens, I accept that brief moment
gratefully, knowing there may be no other--
that for some it will never come at all.

YOUR MOTHER WEARS GOLD LAME COMBAT BOOTS

Flaunt your ego if you have one
gone to party and not the dogs
in flamboyant toggery and startling eyes
egged on by what the others claim to be
but do them all one better.
Decline the obvious like female birds
avoid the mystery at all cost
(mostly when it comes to looks)
take if you can the longer view
screw the deities
peruse outdated Scientific Americans
and trust no one wearing running shoes
nor those too ugly to leave their hair alone
seen with skinny arms in discos
because it ever follows that
what you are is the way you look.

REVIEW

In my dream I am critiquing
the photography of the dream
faulting the composition of the picture
showing you and me
fooling around in front of Mt. Rushmore
scenes when the camera pans too fast
as we travel from Detroit
to indifference.
Even the parts in perfect focus
lack color contrast
and tend to fade into a monotone
with the background more eye catching
than the subject. Our smiles
as we look directly into the lens
are self conscious
and we say our lines like amateurs
not perfectly memorized
spoken perfunctorily as if
our arguments will be forgotten
if we don't rush our words.
The review continues
when I awake and realize
the editing is not well done;
too much ends up
on the cutting room-floor.

IMMORTALITY

When old man Pinzon passes on
he won't just cease; he'll be remembered
for weeks by the worms, a generation
of much obliged microbes, and anyone else
who bothers to notice his tombstone
no more than a pause in the graveyard.
His family will always recall him
seeing themselves in their mirrors
as not fat but quite pleasingly
obese, and his features
will survive as those of his offspring.
Affection and discipline lavished in life
will outlast him as long as the living
recall them or according to their lights
allow them a place in their lifestyles.
His bequest to posterity
will include his apartment
(rent paid to the end of the month)
an overtaxed income and furniture
for a time enough to survive on
and a few weeks' employment for tailors.
He will leave as his legacy
his quips and his teases
La Familia Pinzon drawn by an innocent artist
and the musings of one minor poet.

HOMING

This--a beautiful way to pass
with no tall steeple, no graveyard mourning.
Once-green woods burn their mysteries away.
Heavily harvested fields stretch to the hills
yawning, turning towards their rest. Lakes lie
flat in their beds, cottages retiring--
the last one turning off its light.

Night cuddles in along the shore,
blankets the hills to their necks
darkening the sentinel trees to silhouettes.
The crystal moon shatters into tiny shards
scattered against the sky hovering over sleep.
Silence is broken only by the restless leaves,
the sudden calls of night birds preying.

SEASON'S END

Denise Martinson

About the Author

DENISE MARTINSON

It was during the early years of the Viet Nam War when Denise Martinson wrote her first poem. For a sixteen-year-old girl "war" seemed to ease some of her questions during this trying time. A time when John F. Kennedy, the Beatles, the first man on the moon, and everything else that signified the sixties took hold and ultimately awakened her sense of curiosity. Questions were forever on her mind about life, death, and all the other fundamental things poets ask through their poetry.

She felt by writing poetry she could capture the illusive muse and write subjects that touch both her heart and mind. She says that most poetry written today is blended with reality, then woven with a rich fabric of fantasy--producing both entertainment and food-for-thought for the audience. Denise writes both MIND poems and HEART poems. Her favorite are the MIND poems. Poems that make the reader delve deep into the work, see more than what is written. Even she admits that there are no easy answers in her poetry. Just something to think about. Each poem is a story in itself, a walk through a poet's world.

Denise edits Poetic Page magazine, has two chapbooks, and co-authored a poetry book with Ruth Carol. Her poems and articles have appeared in numerous publications, including stories for the children's market. She is listed in POETS AND WRITERS and has been named in a number of Who's Who books both here and abroad. She says:

> *"We are learning, all of us. We never stop. The wordweaver weaves his words, shapes each sentence to fit the whole. But the perfect poem will never be written because no one knows what perfection is, no one ever will."*

CONTENTS

SYMPHONY _____ 2
THAT WHICH IS WORLDLY _____ 3
PERFECTION _____ 4
GLADIATOR _____ 4
COMPLICATIONS _____ 5
NO MAN'S LAND _____ 6
SUDDEN RIPPLES IN AN ORCHARD _____ 7
SUDDEN IMPACT _____ 8
CAUSES _____ 9
WHEN KNIGHTHOOD WAS IN FLOWER _____ 10
TEMPLE OF THE SOUL _____ 11
ESCAPING GRAY_____ 12
THE SECOND COMING
        IN THE YEAR 2000 _____ 13
ON SEEING MY FATHER
        IN A V.A. HOSPITAL _____ 14
NIGHT COMES WITH BLUE CHARACTERS _____ 15
SHERRY_____ 16
EDWARD SCISSORHANDS _____ 17
OVERTURE OF ABORTIVE MEASURE _____ 18
FUNGUS FEEDING ON OLD WOOD _____ 18
LAND OF THE BRAVE _____ 19
ON COMMON GROUND _____ 20
WATCHING _____ 20
CONFESSION _____ 21
STAR STRUCK _____ 22
CASTAWAYS _____ 23
END THOUGHT _____ 24

SYMPHONY

The crowded mass of trees
rearing leafless crests,
stretch their boughs
like a candelabra;
specters in black robes.
A mist rises from their depths,
turning gold, like a filmy
fairy veil in morning light.
Iridescent spray wets the elms
and ash trees, glittering
like a thousand tiny metal spears.
Mountain primrose raises its
pink crown, and the white
ranunculus spreads its corolla,
so delicate that a mere whisper
of wind rustles their leaves.
Under the soft willows, born
of the great winter silence,
the sobbing of waterfalls
nourishes the first
timid blades of grass.

Award from *WIDE OPEN MAGAZINE*.

THAT WHICH IS WORLDLY

Night pulls
Cleopatra's gown
to conceal every
naked wound she wears,
pins a golden crown
on her hair and sweeps
star dust from her eyes.
But her heart stays pure,
compelled to love
as she never loved before.

Oh, ill-fated queen
with eyes as black
as night, and lips
as wet as the Nile,
does day remove your
scars when Antony's near?
Let not the bite
of death proclaim
you less than what you are:
A woman of the world.

PERFECTION

The Rose

Red petals of softness,
bruised by the thorn.
Perhaps one missing leaf.
A petal curled too much.
Did not God create
the pattern
which roses were to follow?

Then blame the flower, the beetle,
or the wrath of the wind,
but do not blame God.

Roses are fragile.

Published in *Poet's Newsletter.*

GLADIATOR

You cut our love adz-shaped,
sharper than any tongue.
But you see, I don't care.
It takes a true lover of steel
to slice a piece of my heart
and feed it to the lions.
In all fairness to us —
it would be better to kill me
cleanly   than love me at all.

COMPLICATIONS

Leave the door locked, lose the key
as the morning light warms us inside.
Listen...
the windsong soon takes wings and
dances against the window.
Gushing torrents of rain washes off
yesterday's muddy residue;
and glistening drops pearled on leaves
softens our daydreams.
Perhaps if we stay within this storm,
our floundering past will wash away.

Published in *Night Roses.*

NO MAN'S LAND

No man dare caress the rose,
her long, slender thighs;
nor kiss the ruby arms
that unfold each time she feels
his breath against her neck.

No man dare stoop to smell
her scent she sends in silence;
nor drink her beauty
to quench his thirst.

For the harsh wrath of thorns
deny his touch; just as
each drop of blood
dissolves his tears.

Thus, petals soon lie silent on the ground,
where sharp pruning shears are found.

Published in *Bell's Letters*.

SUDDEN RIPPLES IN AN ORCHARD

I am breathless
from your touch:
your hot lips
against my skin,
the way your eyes
grip pieces of my
soul, absorbed
like fresh fruit
when savored whole.

I am breathless
from each succulent
peach you pick,
each warm embrace.
But sometimes love
deceives, and I know...
at the first sign
of rain,   I drown.

SUDDEN IMPACT

Wipe away the tears
Let memories attend
To your sorrows
Like rich desserts
Cascading
The wall you built
Where loneliness feasts.
Eat of its fruit,
For it sweetens
The bitter taste
Left from his death.
Then stop,   briefly
to savor what remains of him.
You know...
That sort, silvery light
On your face.

Published in *Writers Haven Journal.*
(Writer's Bookstore & Haven)

CAUSES

Streaks of lightning and the rumble
of thunder mingled with
the roar of the raging sea.
It left a flicking trail
of light glittering on the rippling waves,
and the wind pushed through
the dense swathes of fog.
Trees along the shore
bent to the wail of birds
beating their wings to safety.
Out of this raging tide
a great plume of snowy spray
shoots across the empty beach,
where exhausted nature seems
to be panting for breath.
The yellow-gray sky
signals the storm to silence.
God's hand intervenes.

10

WHEN KNIGHTHOOD WAS IN FLOWER

Grieving...
She pressed roses to her lips,
veined with secrets she held
like the wind at her throat.
Their red dripped a slim vine
of green over white moiré
where seed pearls threaded satin
on his sword at her feet.

He loved her...to the marrow of her bones,
to the innermost corner of her being...
to her very heart.   He loved her.

Remembering the clink of glasses,
the laughter, the rhythmic clapping
of hands, the fiery wine,
the mythical spirit of midsummer night,
the inevitable disaffection of death——
she knew   heros die hard.

Published in *Words Of Love, Vol. 1.*

TEMPLE OF THE SOUL

As I circle the dirt road
that borders the stately gray structure,
I hear a sighing, peaceful wind
penetrating the stained glass windows.
The door creaks on rusty hinges and latches;
its shutters clacking like old bones.
And the planked floor resists
the weight of a thousand years of guests.
The soft whisper of prayers,
hymns, and hooded saints
echo the drafty hallway.
Lost in the beauty   sins
harbored within   burst free
as I kneel down to pray
on the crumbled stones
        of forgiveness.

Published in *RB's Poets' Viewpoint.*

ESCAPING GRAY

(In Memory of Patricia M. Johnson)

Let me sit beside you
on the shore beyond the grave
and learn the secret of the stars.
Let me hold your hand
and feel the rhythm of the night,
as beat on beat unites.
Does your new life take you
to the poets gone before?
Can you hear their sacred tunes?
Do the delicate sounds of angels
sweeten your lyrical ears?
You...who have dreamed and danced
with the throng of earth poets,
still sing your metrical songs?
Let me walk your garden path,
one last time-
catch the first glint of sun,
and let me touch one final ray
when you sing your hymn,
don silver wings and soar
with the poets of tomorrow.

Published in *Poet's Newsletter*, won
awards from *RB's Viewpoint* and *Mile High.*

THE SECOND COMING
IN THE YEAR 2000

My mind clouded like film
from over exposure.
When it cleared, pictures
raced in technicolor clips
like watered down reflections.

Drifting in and out of sleep
I steal bedraggled hours
to reassess my life.
On learning, I draw a map
at heartache's cost,   wait
to follow directions
where interference reigns.
It takes time, and time
is all I have...

Yet, my egg-shell existence cracks
at the seam, the map shreds
pieces from the whole,
and the world still waits.

ON SEEING MY FATHER
IN A V.A. HOSPITAL

The man on the bed
can't be my father
Not this shrunken face
less full than mine

I watch him
turn his head
try to speak through
thin-cracked lips
      words

I need to hear.

But they die like him
and I think
      they were only
        words.

NIGHT COMES WITH BLUE CHARACTERS

The stars

are out

tonight

and I wonder

if they shine

on the homeless

in the same

light

as they shine

on the blessed.

If not

then I

pray

a falling star

burns a hole

in the sky

for those

who

cross the shining.

SHERRY

Grandma's arms are short,
not long enough for love.
Her last wish was to reach
for the golden ring-
but brass was all she met.
Too many times she left
a trail to nowhere,
going somewhere   for her.
Her only friend was red
red and bittersweet.
Is it any wonder
we found grandma in the cellar-
         no friend in sight,
only her short arms   reaching.

Published in *Verse*.

EDWARD SCISSORHANDS

He usually cuts pieces from the whole,
reveals hidden hearts and love.
Once he found frozen fragments
laced with confusion. A cold
reminder that truth can sting,
burn a dry-ice awareness
on the verge of his extinction.
But he lives and learns,
continues to shape his world
in whatever form fits illusion.

Published in 1993 *Poet's Market*.

(For those who saw the movie.)

OVERTURE OF ABORTIVE MEASURE

Yanked from the throng
of apple trees
then placed on the window sill
hoping for sun.
Never knowing a child's bite,
only the sound of the knife
tearing out its heart.
Feeling the pie dough's clammy
arms squeezing pieces
of pulp and filling
the black hole   ripe
with the season.

Published in *Sisyphus*.

FUNGUS FEEDING ON OLD WOOD

Beneath
the
tide
within
reach
watching
silent
several
day's
growth

LAND OF THE BRAVE

My eyes pierce the night
like arrows aimed at the stars.
My heart beats with the rhythm
of my blood...flowing
in tunneled lakes,   swift
as an eagle's wing,   and
cold. I wear no paint;
dress my wounds in white;
stand like some phantom
against the black tangle
of woods. I hear the earth
shake, feel the vibration
of two-hundred years
rearing death's throes.
It is time, and I know
my people wait in vain
for earth's peace...
and the world knows
we have no solid
vision quests to counter.
Oh, people of the plains,
I tremble for your sons ——
and that which comes after.

Published in *Canto*
Kent State University

ON COMMON GROUND

A trickle of moon
drips crimson
across the starless sky.
Treetops point fingers
as if to accuse the night
of blackout.
Below
howling hell hounds
hunt like predators
devouring their catch,
and the sound of the wind
whispers the devil's name...
wings unfurl, knife-edge death
buried beneath bracken ——
crossless.

Published in *Poetic Page*.

WATCHING

We see ravens perched like sentinels;
their plier-like claws
grip broken branches
where warmth used to sit.
We hear the sound of the wind
brushing black robes--
their rustle, a cold chill.
Someone should have told us
that sentinels are eternal,
that their raucous cry
signifies an ominous death...
ours in the woods
                    for watching.

Published in *Verse*.

CONFESSION

I sit with you when night falls,
and watch the fear in your eyes
hold fast the clock as if
your final hours were spent
holding your son like the time
he hid his half-covered tracks
with newspaper rarely read,
and blood spilled on the
carpet where you lay shot
like a red-tailed hawk screaming
for God or anyone who'd listen,
but who listens to a mother
who never loves or gives a damn
by grabbing her son (by the throat)
and squeezing the trigger finger
of abuse? Not I, not your son,
not God.

STAR STRUCK

For Magic Johnson

On a platform
beneath the flood lights,
        in summer,
we see you turn your head
slightly to the left, knowing
your right side is your best side
in moments like this.
Sometimes shadows interfere
with starry nights, profiles,
and the encompassing mortal world
that reluctantly accepts change
and what it represents:
an immunodeficiency,
unpredictability, a shock wave
of social injustice,   AIDS.

Inside the world of awareness,
you struggle to retire in dignity,
and appoint yourself a worthy
        opponent
to fight the widespread ignorance
of every infected individual.
Once we follow your lead,
        we learn
no anesthetic existence
lacerates a heart more
than when it punctures privilege.

CASTAWAYS

They bend their snowy crowns
like silver-laced sea birds,
searching for Shangri-la.
Half hitched to worn wings,
their Ostrich-like necks
carry the weight of years
with every stooped step they take.
Age has no colored stones
to cast at gray or crashing waves
to wash their rusty plumes;
but flows with the wind
and clouds whatever sun sets
on feeble-minded night...and we,
proud peacocks preen like gods,
forget that we, too, will search
for the "Fountain of Youth"
when we feel the wind's wrath
rage with the rising tide.

For now, we watch
these flightless birds fly--
to wherever their wings take them.

END THOUGHT

My good-bye was casual--no extra
hug, or kiss of sentiment,
which represents love in its
fondest mode, could bring you back.

No irresponsible trumpet's blare
could harold the moment,
more important, than you
in each sweeping note.
(This contradiction is stifling
like the room.   The cause
still shallow with every
miner move.)   God, I miss
you and your caring ways
as I watch the stars
this darkest night.
Hear the sound of distant
ships sail on foggy silence,
and I think.... I see you
under a full moon.   Wonder:
Does death ever hurt
when it, too, cries lonely?

You don't understand.

MEDITATED
SOLITUDE

Patrick Pillars

About the Author

PATRICK PILLARS has been writing stories and poetry since grade school and over the past few years has had numerous poems published in the small press. In 1991 *Unfinished Portrait,* a small chapbook of his poems was published by Wordsmith Publishing Inc.

Patrick, 26, is currently working on a full size perfect bound book of long poems to be published sometime next year. He lives in Saginaw, Michigan with his wife and two sons. They frequently travel around the state to various poetry and art events where Patrick recites his poetry.

As an <u>apprentice publisher and editor</u>--at Wordsmith Publishing Inc.--Patrick's first effort was a beautiful, perfect bound book of poetry by twenty-three Michigan authors entitled, *Poems of the River Junction.*

CONTENTS

ANCIENT ELMS ⎯⎯⎯⎯⎯⎯⎯⎯⎯⎯⎯⎯⎯⎯⎯ 2

QUINN CREEK ⎯⎯⎯⎯⎯⎯⎯⎯⎯⎯⎯⎯⎯⎯⎯ 8

THE HUNT ⎯⎯⎯⎯⎯⎯⎯⎯⎯⎯⎯⎯⎯⎯⎯⎯⎯ 9

MEDITATED SOLITUDE ⎯⎯⎯⎯⎯⎯⎯⎯⎯⎯ 11

FROM HERE TO HERE ⎯⎯⎯⎯⎯⎯⎯⎯⎯⎯ 12

SEASONAL WINDS ⎯⎯⎯⎯⎯⎯⎯⎯⎯⎯⎯⎯ 14

SUNRISE ⎯⎯⎯⎯⎯⎯⎯⎯⎯⎯⎯⎯⎯⎯⎯⎯⎯⎯ 15

SUMMER OF '76 ⎯⎯⎯⎯⎯⎯⎯⎯⎯⎯⎯⎯⎯ 17

OLD MISSION ⎯⎯⎯⎯⎯⎯⎯⎯⎯⎯⎯⎯⎯⎯⎯ 20

SILENT RAGE ⎯⎯⎯⎯⎯⎯⎯⎯⎯⎯⎯⎯⎯⎯⎯ 21

OPENINGS ⎯⎯⎯⎯⎯⎯⎯⎯⎯⎯⎯⎯⎯⎯⎯⎯⎯ 23

ANCIENT ELMS

Wilhelm Borrousch sailed
from Hamburg to Detroit, Michigan
in the long hot summer
of eighteen seventy-five,
bringing his pregnant wife
and German work ethic
to till the rich lands
of New World America.
In spring, he travelled north
to Presque Isle County,
bypassing logging camps
filled with lecherous sin,
to clear a piece of land,
homesteading a family tradition.
The first few years
were filled with harsh winters
and back breaking summers,
building barns and stables,
moving into the house
from the overcrowded soddy,
growing fertile fields,
taming forest to pasture,
rejoicing the wealth of the land.
The state granted the deed
the day he planted the elms,
recording a new beginning.

And the north winds blow
through field and hill,
and the elms sing softly
of the vernal, growing years.

continued

Many years later,
Wilhelm's son Abel
would plant trees
throughout his one fourth
share of the original land,
preserving the natural forest
from hill to shallow swamp.
The devastating Metz fire
during nineteen-ten
destroyed the hill and farm,
killing their baby boy
and countless cattle and pigs
trapped in the burning barns.
Fifteen years later,
after a series of droughts
and long days of rebuilding,
the hill caught fire
during a thunderstorm,
only the rain saved
the house and barns, flattening
the young wheat growing
in the field below.
Again he planted,
rebuilding the house and farm,
but his will was broken
and he died bitter and alone.

And the north winds blow
through field and hill,
and the elms chant softly
in the solstice, longing years.

continued

Walt was a legendary hunter
at the age of twenty-two,
the best rifleman and tracker
in all of Hero township.
At the start of World War II
in nineteen forty-one,
he was working, cutting
timber for extra money,
loading railroad cars
with straight white pine
that was shipped to the war
so many miles away.
The draft board man
lost a son in the woods;
the whole community searched
far and wide for the little
boy, who wandered away
into the deep, dark forest.
Walt hunted and tracked
for three days straight,
only pausing to re-light
his lantern at night
before he found the boy
shivering, afraid and hungry.
He worked the entire war
cutting and shipping timber.

And the north winds blow
through field and hill,
and the elms sigh gently
in the flowing equinox years.

continued

My uncle was twenty
when he waved goodbye
from under the trees, shipping
out to the U.S. Army
he volunteered to serve.
Eight months later,
an official government vehicle
parked under the trees
and two somber officers
broke my grandmother's heart
with news of her son.
Dean was killed over there,
in far off Viet Nam,
fighting bravely with honor,
never losing his faith
and the family's traditional beliefs.
He supported the country
with strong immigrant pride
that still flowed in our
hearts; forgiving, never
forgetting what we live
and die for, always knowing
the sacrifices we make,
living with our choices.
He was the last son
to inherit the family farm.

And the north winds blow
through the field and hill,
and the elms cry softly
of the winter's dying years.

continued

Now as a teenager, I
see what ten years
have left us, and the elms
are rapidly dying of disease,
rotting away, leaving
skeletal branches singing
a death chant to the wind.
The chainsaws shatter
my past with the splitting
echo of trunks severed
from the forgiving soil, marking
the cold wet snow
with tombstones of our past.
I trace each line,
a concentric circle
of my family's history
embedded in the life cycle
of each dead tree.
I remember all the stories
told by my grandparents,
cousins, uncles, and mother;
each story reflected
in the heart of the elm trees
that like all things
given life, have passed
beyond their time.

And the north winds blow
through field and hill,
and memories grow weaker
in the lonely, treeless years.

continued

I have not seen the farm
during my college years,
and did not return
until my second son
was walking and talking.
That spring, my wife
encouraged me to go back
and show her the farm.
As I drove up the hill,
I could see the unplowed
field and overgrown grasses,
the one lane bridge is gone,
replaced by a modern culvert
and the hill looks bare
without those ancient elms.
The falling down barns
and roofless, derelict house
tell her and the two boys
the story of my family.
The boys raced around
the barnyard, playing chase
with butterflies and rabbits
as I told the old stories.
At that moment, I noticed
two green shoots pushing upward,
leaves listening, roots absorbing.

And the north winds blow
through field and hill,
and sapling elms speak softly
in the new age years.

QUINN CREEK

Water washes over silent stones;
the scorpion sun settles in the west.
Shadows grow together, creating a canopy;
golden leaves dance on the cool surface.
Haloed tree tops begin to shimmer and fade;
chameleon reflections turn inevitably gray.

Darkness falls like rich, black velvet;
a frigid sky fills with blinking diamonds.
The moon, streaked with electric blue,
turns ice and snow into cold, hard silver.
Crystal fissures chime in harmony,
while warm spring water flows underneath.

Tall, barren trees etch morning shadows;
ice flows collide under melting sun.
Cardinals and robins wash away winter;
they play and sing in renewed vigor.
Spring buds explode into colorful blossoms;
winter's destruction is strewn with new life.

A warm breeze brings the cool smell of moss;
the lazy creek carries the earth's fragrance.
Dust slides off the vintage, one lane bridge;
trout hide in the shadows of fallen logs.
Footprints begin to fill with liquid mud,
leaving a faint trace of passing thought.

THE HUNT

An orange moon,
shrouded in mist,
slowly descends
into a lavender morning.

A horned owl,
blinking yellow eyes,
trains it's steely gaze
across the barren ground.

The maple tree,
dripping wet snow,
is hard and cold
against my stiff back.

My bare fingers,
aching with frost,
clutch the taut bow
with steady anticipation.

I exhale in the wind
a shallow breath;
the rich cedar
fills me with the earth.

Snow falls from a branch,
marking a secret passing;
signaling the soft approach
of a wild eyed buck.

He steps into the clearing
not thirty yards away;
sniffing the cold wind
for a trace of danger.

continued

He senses a cautious safety,
and breathes easier;
I can feel my impatience
mix with adrenaline.

As I raise the bow,
a primal knowledge
expands from inside,
filling me with the hunt.

At the arrows release,
time slows like mercury;
everything becomes an instant
as my senses are heightened.

My heart beats in rhythm
with the deer's breath,
as the deadly arrow
slips toward our heart.

The buck hears the string
and slowly turns it's head;
eyes of recognition
stare into my soul.

The jagged metal tears
through a momentary peace;
shattering the union
of hunter and prey.

MEDITATED SOLITUDE

A clear sky is filled with stars,
as a full moon rises in the east;
reflections dance across the plain;
vision is measured in light years.

A light snow covers the ground;
warm, spring water shatters the mirror
as harsh winds blow over the lake;
a crystalline symphony drifts outward.

The fireplace glows with warmth,
leaving a trace of burning birch
radiating through shifting images,
and settling into dusty corners.

Cold nibbles at the old solid cabin
in the rising winter solstice;
inside, a consciousness is subdued;
meditated solitude, overshadows all.

FROM HERE TO HERE

I walk across the barnyard
out into the field;
a few scattered leaves
dance across stiff grass.
As I crest the hilltop,
I sit under an old willow;

A full autumn moon rises
clear and bright into a sky
filled with constellations.
Space is filled with a gentle
loneliness, and holds my dreams
as I lose myself in wonder,

and touch the peaceful void;
feeling a quiet communion.
I sense the earth turning,
with each planet a partner,
in the slow , solar dance.
Time slows the rapid river

of my conscious thoughts;
and I begin to visualize
my entire essence soaring,
with my body radiating in an instant
realization of eternal life.
My mind overloads my thoughts

as layers of gray mist
slowly peel away,
revealing a deeper, naked truth;
exposing and uplifting emotions
to explode like supernovas,
and blossom like flowers,

with each petal hinting
at a greater, hidden treasure.
I feel I am ascending
inward and outward, filling
the void with a mystical
song of minimal existence, continued

and fading beyond the abstract
into the pure, ultimate truth.
I rebound off the elemental
essences of the universe,
and swim in the current of God.
Overcome with awe, I slip

back into my own individuality,
and my own, unique presence.
I see my soul beyond time;
then, a single heartbeat
bursts into the present,
and emotion tangles logic;

the gray mist slowly veils
the forgotten, infinite instant.
The reality of my body
flows along the tide
as memory etches experience
into a New understanding,

and I inhale a happiness
that reverberates throughout
my entire existence.
A surety of oneness
breathes a new, fuller life
into my soul, and I feel

magical; no longer alone
in the vast scheme of reality.
A new evolution has begun,
with a knowledge of rightness,
and a stronger, positive faith.
The wind whispers softly;

You are here.

SEASONAL WINDS

Summer's yellowed breath
stains green grasses dry,
igniting errant sparks
into evolutionary fires
quenching Apollo's pyromania.

Autumn's kaleidoscope death
is stripped from trees
by cool, northern winds
that sculpt harvested fields
with aching fingers of frost.

Winter's harsh, biting storms
blow sandpaper snow,
scouring frozen rivers
into mirrored plains
reflecting silent stars.

Spring's trade winds bring
heated days of pleasure
and unexpected growth
with an overdue catharsis
for the melody of the soul.

SUNRISE

From the darkness of the night,
the shimmering constellations fade
in the diffused glow of blue-gray,
washing over the quiet island
in impressionistic watercolors,
as a sliver of yellow-orange

emerges on the distant horizon
splaying subdued shafts of light.
Miles of still blue water
reflect kaleidoscope rainbows
toward wisps of white clouds
with hues of amber and azure,

as the half sun glides upward
with twilight falling behind.
Gentle breezes stir beach grass
in imitation of the waves
breaking the shoreline,
providing rich cymbal washes

to the melody of birdsong
drifting down through trees.
A lone seagull floats in meditation
in a current of warm air,
watching fish rise in answer
to the beckoning call of day;

continued

fingers of golden sunlight
greet the awakening wildlife.
The towering columns of steel,
jutting upward from deep bedrock,
fly flags of shining cable
through the evaporating mist,

exposing barren coastline
in a natural, quiet solitude.
The cool air soothes my mind
as I drink the sunrise
and let the peaceful waves
hypnotize my consciousness,

releasing me of everyday burdens
and allowing me to rest
in nature's cradling arms;
feeling safe in the comfort
of summer's sweet embrace,
escaping to simple paradise.

SUMMER OF '76

The warm June day
blows through trees
in gentle waves of silence.

Putting the kite together;
my brother tests the wind
with paper, string, and wood.

Our kite touches clouds
mingling with birdsong
high above grass and hill.

With wind's awakening pace,
power lines snare our bird,
ending our day bittersweet.

My grandfather wields
a homemade baseball bat
squinting into the sun.

Baseballs soar beyond
the barnyard fence;
my arm growing listless.

We switch places,
Grandpa catching pitiful
grounders from my swings.

Grandpa relives the past,
teaching me fundamentals
older than baseball.

continued

18

The antique cane pole
quivers in the current
of the cool creek.

Using hand-tied flies
with years of fish,
colors skim on the surface.

Lurking brown trout
watch from fallen cedars,
testing childhood patience.

A string of triumph
is worth walking
the long road home.

Confetti and balloons
float through July haze,
coloring parade day.

Every marching band,
classic car and fire truck
passed through town.

Carnival noise and odors
drift through the county fair
enticing and delighting.

The clear night sky
explodes in memory
of pride and perseverance.

continued

Another bale of hay
is stacked amid dust
mixed with summer sweat.

The old farmer's bent back
struggles through the chore
of keeping the farm alive.

Two young city boys
are fascinated by the farm
and the life they miss.

The wagon load is stacked
in the loft of the barn
amid dreams and livelihood.

Cars park on the lawn
where men and boys split
from the women carrying food.

The beer supply dwindles
as men talk business,
pitching worn horseshoes.

The women chat about family,
recipes and babies,
setting a banquet homemade.

The traditional reunion
bonds the diverse family
for a few hours of memories.

OLD MISSION

Honey bees dart between cherry blossoms,
as a cool breeze blows off the lake
with the morning sun trailing behind;
ancient elms trace long shadows of the past.

The clear blue water portrays still life
portraits of the meandering shoreline;
each pebble and stone, an etched history
of the days before man walked here.

A broken shell from the pioneer days
is the only remnant of the mission church,
where brave men brought their message,
leaving their homeland for the new world.

Even the lighthouse at the peninsula's point
has become a relic of long forgotten days,
when severe Michigan storms threw sailboats
against the dangerous limestone reefs.

Orchards and mansions fill the country side
with modern technology and civilization.
This too will pass in the currents of time,
leaving memories and museums of the present.

SILENT RAGE

A soft blue sky
merges with the bay
on the distant horizon.

A cool, refreshing breeze
blows through my hair,
rustling the grassy shore.

I step into the water
that reluctantly clings
to a Michigan winter.

In the distant Bay,
a single, white sail
catches the morning sun.

I'm far away from the river
spewing city sewage
and relentless factory fog.

But this deserted beach
still holds back human
civilization and spoilage.

I can almost imagine
a simple time of wonder,
when Indians lived with nature.

continued

A small reflection catches
my eye below the water,
in the sand at my feet.

From the bottom silt,
I pull out a syringe
covered with algae.

How could this be?
I kick through sand
and find more refuse.

An old Indian Chief
crying on television,
explodes from my memory.

Below serenity,
is a wasteland
washed upon beauty.

Now I understand the tears
and the loss of sacredness;
living with the silent rage.

OPENINGS

A world with walls;
hiding unshared treasures
and keeping out the calls
of the desperately lonely.

Let the garden breathe
spring breezes, and bask
in the shade of trees
in nature's embrace.

Let the children scamper
across the unfettered land,
absorbing rich diversity
in all it's complexity.

Live with the cure
of mind and soul,
by forgetting insecurity
and painful depression.

Look at the sky
beyond the clouds;
wish upon the mighty
stars of promised hope.

continued

In each blade of grass,
feel the planets pulse.
In a high mountain pass,
listen for a peaceful sigh.

Live with logic and emotion
as precious gifts of life
and experience the flow
of love beyond measure.

Know the rhythms of life
as a magical moment;
a union without strife
in the universal chorus.

Break down the barriers
and accept nature's fate.
Live in a world
devoid of any walls.

After the Rain
Comes The Rainbow

Rosemary J. Schmidt

About the Author

ROSEMARY J. SCHMIDT has been a volunteer for most of her life. Having three daughters and four sons, encouraged her to spend more than a dozen years in the scouting program and several years as an assistant 4-H leader. Over the years, nearly a hundred boys and girls spent time in her home learning how to tie knots, make papier-mache, and sing camp songs. She was easily recognized as she drove through the township with a station wagon full of children in uniform. She took those youngsters on such outing as overnight campouts, roller skating, and sledding. Through the scouting program she was able to give her own children an insight into the machinations of the outside world. And of course, she spent countless hours at school with her own children as room mother for field trips, plays, and bake sales. She cooked suppers for the football team, made costumes for school plays, and warmed benches while her children played sports and participated in other school functions.

Rosemary spent many years in the PTA program where she held various offices including the office of Vice-President. Several times a year she could be found at home with those same ladies of the PTA, going over maps and designating areas for Mother's Marches for the March of Dimes, Cancer Society, Muscular Dystrophy, and Drug Abuse.

She spent several years working one and sometimes two days a week helping to "pattern" a brain-damaged child. From that volunteer work came a television program which she produced--about "mainstreaming" mentally handicapped children into the regular school system. As a past member of the Junior Woman's Group she helped to raise money for the Big Sister Program and the Underground Railroad for abused women.

Rosemary has been writing poetry for about 40 years, has been published numerous times in the USA and in Canada. This is her third poetry book to be published, and she has been included in many anthologies around the country. Even in her poetry, she has volunteered by doing free readings at schools, taverns, nursing homes, bookstores, and at prison.

She is the Vice-President and Editor of Wordsmith Publishing, Inc., and has recently retired as editor of The Poets of Now Poetry Magazine. Besides poetry she also writes prose. She and her husband, Ted, co-authored a book on home mortgages several years ago. She hopes to have a novel and several short stories on the market before the end of 1993. Rosemary was born and raised in Saginaw, Michigan, and still resides there.

CONTENTS

STEEL-GRACE _____ 2
APPLESAUCE TEARS _____ 3
THERE'S SOMETHING WRONG WITH AUTUMN _____ 4
IN SHEEP'S CLOTHING _____ 5
THE SHATTERING OF A POSTCARD DAY _____ 6
LILY _____ 7
COMIN' FOR TO CARRY HIM HOME _____ 8
GOIN' HOME _____ 9
PRODIGAL SON _____ 10
INNOCENTLY DETACHED _____ 11
THE LIES THEY TELL _____ 12
PARADOX _____ 13
ABSTRACT TIME _____ 14
FINIS CORONAT OPUS _____ 15
PROVOCATIONS OF A WORKING WOMAN _____ 16
SUMMER'S HEAT _____ 17
FIRST CAR _____ 18
SWEET BABY SWEET _____ 18
MY DARLING _____ 19
LOVE IS _____ 20
OMNIA PRO UNO, ET UNUS PRO OMNIBUS _____ 21
THEY DO RESEMBLE _____ 22
THROUGH THE LOOKING GLASS _____ 23
AN AUTUMN APPLE DAY _____ 24

STEEL-GRACE

"A darkness is formed and a crime is committed.
The fault lies not with the one committing the crime,
but with him who formed the darkness." -VICTOR HUGO-

I sat across from you in English class

You stood out, your demeanor so strangely different
    When the bell rang, you eased out of your seat
    and melted through thirty students lunging at the door
You were not like the rest
    your movements were thought out
    well planned, sharply calculated
I had heard about you
    your weekly rumbles with the gang
    your weapons, your knives, your guns

Your head, cupped in that forever-turtleneck sweater
    bore eyes that flowed around the room
    like hot ebony liquid
Your square, stubby body
    belted with silver studs
    moved in steel-grace,
Your muscular legs stressing faded denim
    melded into worn motorcycle boots that
    clicked heavy on the wooded floor of English class

I had a secret crush on you
    but you walked past me and through me
    as if I were vapor

Autumn stormed our world that year
    As rain pelted leaves to the ground
    you crashed with them
    The news of the day was about the "local" boy
who robbed and stabbed an old woman thirty times

APPLESAUCE TEARS

No invitation for Emmy.
        Julie said, "Come anyway."

Julie's mother said,
        "No room" ——
                handed her a bag of apples;
                shut the door.

Emmy stood on the porch,
        holding the apples,
                listening to the party
        on the other side of the door.

There came a big burning hole
        where her stomach ought to be.

Down the steps ——
        out to the sidewalk ——
                the hole closed up
        and her stomach came back.

To the grass and to the trees and to the
        cracks-that-break-your-mother's-back ——
........she said, "I don't care, I hate Julie anyway."

She pitched the apples into the street ——
                cars turn them into applesauce.

THERE'S SOMETHING WRONG WITH AUTUMN

Summer seeps in an open window
to warm the child's face.
Daddy dances her 'round the room,
singing, "Put your arms around me, Honey, hold me tight".
He loves her--she knows he loves her...
She feels warm-happy-safe.

Suddenly she's sitting in a pile of crunchy leaves.
The air smells different... cold.
A razor-like crack explodes from the house slicing the autumn air.
Mother, splattered with blood, stumbles down the steps
to drag the child from the leaves like a Raggedy Ann.

Today there are no more remembrances of daddy,
no more dancing 'round the room,
no more, "Put your arms around me, Honey, hold me tight".
And every year there's something wrong with autumn.

5

5

IN SHEEP'S CLOTHING

Spring's tender leaves dance shadows
on large, flat stones
shaped like crosses and lambs
that remind her of bible stories

The car smelling of tobacco
parks near the stones
decorated with flowers
that smell like mother's dressing table

The man's voice rings hollow and strange
       "Take off your panties, put them here"
She stands on the seat, rubbing the spot
       With the toe of her shoe

Getting out of the car with silver coins in her hand
       she hears the voice, "If you tell, I'll cut off your legs"
       She runs-falls-wails
       across velvet lawn to mother's arms

Mother says, "You're not hurt, you hardly fell
              hardly fell
                  fell"

THE SHATTERING OF A POST CARD DAY

Wild flowers nod to
      fields of waving wheat.
Clouds, too perfect, pass on by
      as warm sun and cool breezes
         comb the earth.
Dust funnels follow farm tractors
      as cow tails swish away flies.
The old church, parishioner poor,
      bears the shame of uncut lawn.
A train whistle sounds in the distance--
      then nearer--
         nearer to a stalled yellow bus--

Twenty-one sixth graders watch in horror
      as metal scrapes metal.

LILY

Remember the day, Lily...

We played that game, remember?
You and I, we did.
You chanced to fall
And hurt your head.
I cried. My tears were hid,
But I cried for you.
The blood was scarlet
Against your face so white.
I thought sure you were dead,
But you opened your eyes
And looked at me.
I carried you home, Lily,
And laid you on the bed.
Your blond curls, matted with blood
Lay stiff against the satin pillow.
You reached out with tiny hand
And touched my cheek;
That's when my tears began to spill.
You said, "...my brother" and
Closed your eyes forever.

Lily, I roam the fields no more,
And games are gone forever,
But, I'll never let go of your smile;
It's imprinted on my heart.
You were only six and I twelve,
But, I loved you, Lily,
And now you're gone.

COMIN' FOR TO CARRY HIM HOME

The old man
       and he still full of years
            strolled the beach
       as wing-ed angels hovered near

Their idle talk kept beat
       to waves that gently
            strummed the shore
       as wing-ed angels softly hummed

The old man knew
       of life and broken dreams
            but he still full of years
            held Grandpa's hand
            to speak of dreams unfolding yet
       as wing-ed angels sang of promised land

The old man knew the way of dreams
       the things of which life sometimes seems
            things he could not speak
            to child fair and sweet
       as wing-ed angels bid him come

Little hands
       lifted shell
            to Grandpa's ear
       as wing-ed angels hushed the air

"Grandpa! Listen to the shell
       It sounds like angels calling out"

Wing-ed angels bid him hurry as
                they fluttered thereabout

GOIN' HOME

So-long, Charlie,
I'm tired and I'm
           goin' home.
I've run the road,
I'm gettin' old,
I'm headin' home
           to get some rest.
I've seen it all,
           I've met the best.
To hell with all the rest.
I'm tired, Charlie,
Don't ask me to stay.
There just ain't no way.

I've tried it all, Charlie,
And now I'm goin' home.
Don't wag your tail
           ol' man,
It won't do you any good.
I said I was goin' home,
And that's what I meant.
So-long, Charlie.
I don't know if they'll
           let you in...
But just in case...
I'll see you there.
So-long, Charlie.

PRODIGAL SON

He came with bated breath
To languish at my door
He stood
      waiting
            just waiting
For me to invite him in
He spoke but never said a word
      tears welled up against the brown
      then on his cheeks they pelted down
      down
         down
I wanted to say come in, come back
      but I knew he could not
         would not stand
            if I held him up
I shook my head
He turned and left
      Pain stabbed at me
      as he lingered on the walk
Turning back, he searched my eyes
      Once more I shook my head

I turned around
      Now it was I
      whose tears were falling down
      down
         down
The nights thereafter
      were long, so long
I cried, I prayed, I cried some more
      I could not help my son

He traveled roads that were hard
      roads that were long and wrong
but always wrapped tightly in my prayer,
      he traveled along

Then my prodigal son came home

INNOCENTLY DETACHED

Kathy! Oh, Kathy!
You've done it again.
You told me you wouldn't,
but now you have.

Kathy said nothing,
But stared straight ahead,
Her dark hair matted
Against white shiny face.

How many times, Kathy,
Do you have to be told,
To stay where I put you
And not move at all?

Kathy just sat there,
Her expression bland,
Blue eyes flickered
In light overhead.

The little girl gently
Lifted Kathy to her breast,
and curiously examined
The doll's broken leg.

THE LIES THEY TELL

On this night of loneliness,
I stand here proud as dust.
I wonder where's tomorrow,
For they promised it would come.
Oh, Yes! They promised.
And it's always there in sight,
But, as the sun unfolds itself
They tell me it's today.
My dreams are locked up in
            Tomorrow;
My tears are in today.
So, as I know tomorrow,
My dreams will never come.

WINTER BIRD

Flitting to feeder
He pecks the solid hunk
      Of frozen feed
To break loose
One little morsel.
His flights are short;
From feeder
To naked sugar maple
Then back again.

Will his feathered
Little body
Survive the cold?

Or does life end
On a frosty branch?

PARADOX

The unexplained
Mystifies the soul.

The inner mind
Cannot accept;
It delves and delves
Into the predicament.

Soon the soul is in
A wrath of turmoil,
And the mind
In complete agony...

For it seems
A paradox that...

We first must die
To live again.
To save our life
We must give it up,
Because all we keep
We're sure to lose,
But what we give,
We more than receive.

ABSTRACT TIME

Each day
    I look behind me
    to view the past
An invisible wall
    keeps me out
I want to go back
    change things
But the wall detains me
I must go forward
Into unexplored time
    I know not
    what I will find
    or feel
I'm told not to look back
    to forget the past
    but I cannot
    I cling to it
For I know that the key
    to the future
    lies in the past
I scrutinize each detail
    of the future
Holding it up to the past
    paring away at flaws
    polishing each facet
Until it reflects a panorama of color
    as prisms in sunlight

But each examination
    becomes the past and soon
    I get caught up in past things
The future suffers
    it cannot happen
    in its rightful order
Because with magnifying glass
    I amplify the past

Oh, but that I could have
    past and present side by side
    to run a race, to win a laurel
But instead I go two steps forward
    and one step back

FINIS CORONAT OPUS

(The end crowns the work)

In the day and in the night
The angels sing above the ground,
And in the day and in the night
Their heavenly voices abound
As they spin around and fly on down
To pick another rose.

So when I die, just turn me loose
In garden high and wide.
Let me fly with wings of gold,
And let it be my choice
To fly... to fly so bold...
My worldly friends rejoice,
For if I've left what I came to leave,
Then please rejoice at my reprieve.

I've worked so hard and I know why,
But, now I want to fly
With writers of the past;
Chaucer, Gibran, Steinbeck, Hugo...
Just to name a few.
So now, just set me free, and let me be,
Let me fly in the great divine...
For there, my friends, I'll visit you
When you come nigh in time.

And when you do, we'll play a game
Of ring-around-the-rosie
As children often do.
We won't be embarrassed to play in the sun
When time is up and day is done.
With laurels in our hair and music in the air,
We'll join our hands and fly around
To sing in joyful sounds.
We'll dance, my friends,
We'll sing and laugh; and when the day is through,
I'll rest with you.
So cry not now, my friends
As I go yonder-place to fly.
Good-bye, good-bye, good-bye.

PROVOCATIONS OF A WORKING WOMAN

One day you wake up and wonder
what if life is like the clock
sixty seconds, sixty minutes
sixty years

There's so much to see
and so much to do
The tickety-tocks are getting closer

Hurry, hurry! You feel like
the proverbial white rabbit of
Alice in Wonderland

A shopping trip; this life
I can't afford, don't need, and don't want!
Keep it, take it back

No frills, no glitter, no pomp
and circumstance - and most definitely
no useless tidbits

Bones brittle, tired, rusty
creaky
only taking
what I can carry
on my back
Don't load me down with useless
WEIGHT

SUMMER'S HEAT

The summer's hot breath
Has melted the asphalt;
The catch basins are steaming;
Traffic has slowed to a lull.
But, there in the midst of the
Burning sun stands the great
Blue Spruce looking like it just
Stepped out of a winter's scene...
Cool and refreshing as though its
Branches had been dipped in frost.
The *Honey Locusts* are spreading their
Delicate leaves across the street
To blot out the sun with a lacy veil.
The *Northern Catalpas* stand tough and hard;
Their broad leaves defying the glaring sun;
Causing envy to the *Mountain Ash*,
Whose warm clusters of orange seem to
Draw the heat of summer.
The *Great Oaks* demand respect as they
Tower over the rest. The *Norway Maples,*
Even in their dark dress, refuse to
Accept the summer's hot rays. And all the
Other trees, nameless in my mind,
Stand waving leafy branches at
A multitude of birds flying high above
The earth... They're nameless, too,
Except for the fat little housewives...
The *Mourning Doves.*

FIRST CAR
For Ted Jr.

Three hundred dollars,
A sixteen year old boy,
And the hunt is on.

Old Corvairs without backseats
Trucks without engines
And rust-coated station wagons,

That one's a gas hog
This one burns oil
Ten buck less
And that's a deal?

Missing batteries
Rusty cavities
Bald tires
And tears in his eyes

Three hundred dollars
Will buy nothing but derelicts
In the Sargasso sea
Of Saginaw, Michigan.

SWEET BABY, SWEET
For Audrey

Silky blond hair
Frames cherub face
Like clusters of down.
Bright, shining eyes,
Spring water blue,
Sparkle in morning sun.
Miniature hands
Make a fist
Into rosebud mouth.
Fawn-like chin
Glistens with infant drool.
Chubby, pink cheeks;
Softer than soft.
To you
I sing a lullaby,
Sweet baby, sweet.

MY DARLING
For Ted, Sr

The grey lines your temples;
A crown of glory.
You've worked for it,
You've earned it,
And it's beautiful.
You're not the young man I married
You're a thousand times better.
You still remember to kiss me
Hello and good-bye,
(and sometimes sneak one from behind).

You make me feel like a woman,
A woman loved.
And, so, my darling,
With each passing day,
How can I help but love you
Just a little bit more?

LOVE IS

Like a cool running brook
That washes over me
To cleanse my soul
With sacred water

It's like fire, hot and painful
That burns my tender heart
To make me pliant
in my lover's hands

It's like the great winds of the North
That rip at my being
Making me naked
And vulnerable

It's like a jagged rock slide
That tumbles me apart
To cut my soul...
But, I bleed willingly

OMNIA PRO UNO, ET UNOS PRO OMNIBUS
(One For All, And All For One)

As the Phoenix ascends from
       the funeral pile
       to rise from its ashes
       in the freshness of youth

So, too, the students of OMNI---
       in our omniumgatherum
       of caring, of vision, of mission
       we rise beyond shattered esteems

We rise---we rise to a new cycle
       of greatness, of compassion, of understanding
       knowing that as all things change
       we too must change

We learn new things, we gain awareness
       we fling aside the old
       and take on the emblem of immortality
       in our education--in our lives

No more can the world look down
       for we are a new breed
       we have visions and dreams
       we march into a new mission

Out of the ashes of ignorance
               we have risen!

This poem was written for the **ACT OMNI**   Adult High School graduating class of Saginaw county, 1992.

THEY DO RESEMBLE

God took his cookie cutters out,
A dozen or so.
He looked them over,
And chose just one.

With hands so deft
He patted the dough,
Then cut one here,
And cut one there.

As He picked them up,
He stretched one long,
And squashed one short.
With one swift slash
There came a variety of mouths.
Another quick dash,
A wide range of eyes.
A pinch here, a push there,
And noses, what noses!

They raised and baked
And came alive...

Those cookie-cutter people
The Lord hath made.

THROUGH THE LOOKING GLASS

As a suckling babe
        I knew not but comfort, warmth, hunger
I progressed
        a waddling child
                romping through life
                touching hot things
                learning not to
Adolescence brought
        a thousand seeds of knowledge
        I watered them daily
        fed them
Then crisis after crisis --
        the generation below wanted to grow up
        the generation above passed away
Middle age continued to creep forward
        pulling at my flesh
                blurring my eyesight
                adding poundage to my weight
My reflection stares back
        in horror, in pain, in humor
        but always in love
I have one more step into the looking glass
        that of old age
        I have prepared for that season
                by collecting memories
                that will sustain me till the time
                when I enter into the Kingdom
                        to reign
                        with Him
                              who will make me perfect

AN AUTUMN APPLE DAY

I walked along a country road--
       sandy soil sifted through my sandals;
              cornfields rustled all around--
                    over-ripe and brown.

I passed some stalwart cows
       standing in a sunlit field.
              I stopped to say hello--
          The dairy queens, all brown,
              stared at me with chocolate eyes
                    then sauntered off to graze.

A nearby apple tree
       beckoned me to come--
              to have a tasty treat--
       I tiptoed through
          the thicket
              to pick a juicy jewel.

I've eaten apples all year long--
through the years--come and gone,
              but I must confess,
              the autumn apple is the best.

Passepartout Chanson

Christopher Corbett-Fiacco

About the Author

CHRISTOPHER CORBETT-FIACCO was born in upstate New York on April 2, 1961, one day too late to accurately account for an oft-expressed self-description as an April Fool. The new back porch for which his parents had been saving at the time was supplanted by a matched set of cribs for the twin boys who arrived on Easter Sunday. His folks have always insisted the twins were the better investment. Four brothers preceded and one followed in a household of seven boys and four bedrooms (one bathroom). "It can be awful for a kid to grow up in a big family, but wonderful for an adult to have grown up in one. If it's done right, you end up with a fistful of lifelong friends you know you'll never lose."

In 1985, Chris legally changed his surname so as to couple his mother's family name and heritage with that of his father's. "Your name is like a title by which others come to know you, and I wanted my title to accurately reflect both branches of the tree on which I sprouted and was nurtured. Besides which, I think it looks great in print."

Chris has had dozens of poems and a couple of short stories published in such magazines and anthologies as *The Archer, Back Alley Review, The Chiron Review, Fennel Stalk, Frugal Chariot, Kana, Pegasus,* the Amherst Society's *American Poetry Annual,* and *Vandeloecht's Fiction Magazine.* His fourth first novel is making the rounds of literary agents, and his first second novel is underway. Since 1990, Chris has edited and published the quarterly literary magazine **SISYPHUS**. Having lived in Boston for a decade, Chris expects a move to the Pacific Northwest sometime in the coming year.

CONTENTS

BLUE SKY _____ 2
lionheart _____ 3
PASSEPARTOUT CHANSON _____ 4
LOVE'S ELEGY_____ 5
FORTUNE COOKIE _____ 6
SAFARI _____ 6
unknown _____ 6
PRELUDE _____ 7
honor _____ 8
PARLEZ VOUS _____ 10
DESERT NIGHTS _____ 11
dark shadow _____ 12
NOW WITNESS _____ 13
BECAUSE I NEVER MET YOU _____ 14
FIRST LOVE POEM FOR YOU _____ 15
touch _____ 16
skylark _____ 16
love is a rose _____ 16
CAPTAIN COMFORT _____ 17
crystal _____ 17
keeper of the bones _____ 18
hurricane _____ 19
after the dance _____ 20
UNTITLED SEVENTH REQUIEM _____ 20
interpretation _____ 21
ADULT EDUCATION _____ 22
THE WEDDING POEM _____ 24

BLUE SKY

poem for my mother

Blue sky, soft in morning
like my mother's arms
who cradled me
from tears,
the gentle love,
her warm protection
I would crawl into
and hide me from my fears.

Blue sky, misted
like her eyes in memories
in lonely nights,
her quiet hush in lullabies
who kissed me off to sleep.

In dream I wander
back to her
and listen for her heart.
In dream I've said
I love you
every day of my life.

Blue sky
on a rainy Sunday morning,
bring me back to mother's love
and sweet October smiles
of her eyes.

lionheart

later,
i am
old enough to see what
no son
hidden in the underbrush of
evanescent shadow can
aver; how from the quiet voice is born a
rhythmic echo, ever faithful; how in the gentle hand
there is the strength of shelter.

PASSEPARTOUT CHANSON
for Michael

How the night lay full
your promises of dream,
vagrom visions;
eyes move slowly
from the darkness to the darkness
of your hollow room,
your empty brain; silent heart
a lone companion
through your passages of time.

Across your vision
suddenlike
across the night sky
gloaming fireflies of dream
alight like stars
your bloodtide swells
against the moon and breaks
against the stone of this captivity.

Now you listen for your starsong
(distant chimes
  cosmos converging
  god-like in the galaxies)
you hear
the soft low hum of whispered incantations
from the lips of ancients
sifting through these mists of time
like strands of summer breeze that
brush your cheek that
kiss you from the clouds.
Softlight now your melodies in night
and no one else can hear them

continued

but you

Passing
riddles without meaning
secret messages nor truths to hold
you
find your own
time moving
quickly
slowly

quickly
minutes into hours into days
gone down to starlight
and a glimmer of a smile
(that which passes and allows your passage
  through).

Will you sing but softly;
you will know the words.

LOVE'S ELEGY

Once
I reached up to kiss your eyes
and tasted you

seeping from them.

FORTUNE COOKIE

A Smile is Your Welcome Mat

don't mean you can wipe your
climbing boots on my face.

SAFARI

Brushing me from your skin
like picking cat hairs from your sleeve
and you are off on secret journeys

leaving not a scent
to tempt the lonely
lap hound.

unknown

understand it was
never my intent to
keep you always
naked in the wings
of my nightplay. but you
wouldn't dress the part. and you
never read your lines as they were written.

PRELUDE

how you come at me
in little hours of the night,
such accusations, questions

(I disclose myself in code,
  never really thinking
  I can fool you).   you

who are a part of me
I cannot lay at rest
(as if I've tried).
Let me sleep awhile;
I will hold in dream no secret.

in the rain I hear you weep
for my desires.
in the morning you'll unburden me of silence.

but for now it is enough to feel
your eyes strip off my skin.
enough
to know your crippled gaze
and listen to your cold wise admonitions.

honor

shattered
by a sudden restless movement
(you against your sleep or me
  against you)

cold dawn like a mirror hung
above our dead night
comes down hard
on us like
shattered

shards of shadowed morning
raining heavy
splintered light
that slices through the underbelly
of my white fear
(cutting clean the flesh of dream
  from cold bone of reality);

sharp-edged as regret.

stumbling from the wreckage of my sleep and you
in my eyes, all I know
are bald reflections
of our days of sickness
and the silent midnight
rage of love
who's dying in my arms.
(thrashing in this deathbed
 crying out in pain
 I could so carelessly ignore
 its tortured passions
 but for silences of sorry eyes
 who beg my every miscast glance;

come,
love,
I will rock you
gently
into that sleep.)

what poetry there's left in us
is written in a language lost
(the scratching of your touch
  against the cold damp underwall
  of my hard skin).
undeciphered
in the grotto of my heart
what poetry there's left in us is

disregarded in the headlines
of the pages
of the news
and real estate appraisals
and the comics.
now you greet me like your danish
and you wipe away the taste of me
as you go on to
editorials.

and I turn away from you
again and dream
of blue stars, other lovers' arms and sad goodbyes,
sight of strangers' eyes in dark rain from outside
my window

crash of shattered glass
and torn regret
(my great escape).

alone
unlike myself
unlike our love
my many poems have their honor.
you will not discredit them.

and I will not dishonor you.

PARLEZ VOUS

Eyes alone may speak this language,
understand a tale of how the heart once blossomed full
beneath your touch
lay now as barren under bald moon, withered,
weeping.

There are not words that move through thicknesses of silences
like these
to speak of whispers careful on my neck in night
as prayers that fed my hungry soul,

nor tell of how your breath like oxygen to my mouth
came
when I in orphaned afterbirth lay
bruised and bloodied
wasting at the teat of desecration
and as foundling suckled at the nipple of your mercy.

There is no saying how you cradled me
and taught me what is life
and what is love
and how to know the difference.

Eyes alone may speak it.
Eyes alone will understand the tale
and tell you I have come to learn the difference.

And there is life.

DESERT NIGHTS

alone again,
except for me;

a desert flower
flush with bud

anticipating sun

but with no wind or rain
caressing
I may flourish for a day
or more

and fear the cold hard eyes of night
will watch me
wither slowly
down to death

alone
again

(except for me).

dark shadow

lonely cries the sparrow in her doom,
her broken flight through darkened skies,

her lover gone across the moon,

her drizzling night through cat eyes
opened full

and watching from my room
I dare not lift my shadow to her call.

oh
sweet melancholy echo of my heart,
whose song like sad confinement
bears no honor in the rain,
her heavy wings no use
against the razored claws of time;

how I bear my darkest joy at her surrender.

NOW WITNESS

Come midnight rain
and chill wind shifting restless at the pane
as brain that reaches
green and foggy like the lowland,
heart as bloody-bruised in torment,
raw as sky is stained;
I waken as if waiting at command.

Was not alone in dream I felt her
leave my bed again, nor in dream rose up heedless
groping grievous for her hand.
Come waking rain
a dank wind shifts relentless at my pane;
I am again as subject fallen hard beneath her restless reign;
I follow, yet I do not understand.

Would she betray what bane has bound her
savage at the chain that shackles her heart
like a sinner seeking grace, confessing blame;
or name that demon twisting tortured torment from her shame;
or rail against a penance that would maim;
I might as simple as a savior wipe away the stain of tear
that trembles in her eye; caress her pain.
But she cannot destroy what only order has been lain,
nor tempt such fate in vain, nor quick deny.
Now witness cast, I do not hope to vie.

Would she look back she could not catch me
weeping for her claim,
nor turning
glimpse these yearning eyes inflame.
Should she return she would not feel me
burning for her charm.
I have come myself to harm

and lay as lame.

BECAUSE I NEVER MET YOU

doesn't mean I never loved you.
From first-sight spied in lonely night-watch
have I loved you
blindly
without recourse,
without mission.

Because I never said hello

is not a testament that we have never
spoken
in the languages of intrigue.
Through the smokey haze of celebration
every gesture is a clue;
every move a mystery
revealed.

Because I never touched you

is not reason to presume
I cannot know the soft caress of your flesh
pressing hard against me.
My eyes have made love to you
long amid the restless pulse of neon
mirrored in recesses of this place.

Because I never promised you my heart

is not to say that you don't carry it
precariously so, unmindful
of what torment or what ecstacy I'd suffer
for the hunger of the lover
I will never know

because I never met you.

FIRST LOVE POEM FOR YOU
(your name goes here)

you told me
in your own way
that you want a poem.
written for you. love
and everything like life
put down in ink, you said.
your name scribbled into title,
immortalized
in word. (immortalized
  on paper
  in a binder that lies on my desk,
  sometimes open.)
you said

it must be wonderful. a poem
written for you. dedicated to you.
no one ever has
before. a poem
and the world would know.
(how do I tell you that
  the world does not read the binder
  that lies on my desk,
  sometimes open?)
but you said

it must be wonderful.
a poem. for you.
you said it so clear,
even with your eyes.

so here it is, a poem
for you.

I hope you like it.

touch

tell me
only that you
understand the
chaos of the hopeless heart.
help me. lie if you have to. help.

skylark
  for Ramón

seeking
kindred of the
yarrow was I
lonely-muted loveless sparrow
angry-marked by scars of old
regret and wounded wing.
kingfisher come alight, I take to flight and sing.

love is a rose

I'd brave a bushelful of thorns
for a petal
of your love.

CAPTAIN COMFORT

Captain, was a time I might have turned my eyes
Away.
Pretender
To the throne of independence I was
All the time pretending
I could do for me.
Never a wistful wit to needing anyone again.

Chance is all we owe
Our thanks to.
Maybe for a missed glance I would not have
Found you. Maybe you would not have tried again.
Oil on the chain, that's what you are to me now.
Riding rapture into sunset, how I think of us.
Trading tears for kisses, cant for comfort, you become my heart.

crystal

could I ever hope to
render verse delicious as
your candied kiss, or
satisfy the craving of the blind
tongue calling through
a dark night hungry as the
lonesome poet suckled on a crag?

keeper of the bones

that's who you are. you
who finger marrow; taste
my blood.
I am secretive and indiscreet.
I am hard as hunger. Insatiate,
you mine the hollows of me,
skin me
stripping flesh from meat from
muscle down to
bone, discarding much.
vegetarian. you chew
at my remainder like an old
dog, bury me
beneath your bedpost, reconstruct
the shell of who I might have
been;
catalogue what fractures
there have come.

hurricane

how you came; me
under bald eye,
ripened in the whorling
restless rampage of sundry nights.
i with a small i
cannot even yet
assume what's natural and not
natural; and what an
evanescent shadow of a wild wind melting down along the outer wall.

after the dance
(Fourth Requiem for Jackson Pollock)

kneeling
unkissed
here your dancer
burned like afterbirth
or consequences
expectations
hidden in the vestments of his honor.

relentless
love blossomed.

UNTITLED SEVENTH REQUIEM
for Jackson Pollock

fifteenth
window up
I saw him
powerless
as prayer
blackpoem
nightsong
or a poet
silent as
survivors
left with
not a wit
to keying
portraits
tarnished
colorless
as virtue
faithless
as intent

interpretation

it was sometime in the
night
they came to me in voices bruised with fear and envy
even as I slept they called
repeating
poetries of reckless rhyme and little
reason
every
tattered phrase
a turgid tale of tortured testament
temptation
issued like command
or veiled like invitation terrored as a
nightcry echoed hard against the slumber of the deafmute.

Adult Education

(based on a poem by Mark Greeley)

There is a difference
between grasping a hand
and seizing a soul.
There is a difference

between catching a smile
and capturing contentment.
After a while
you see that

love is no teacher
and you are
a student of love.
After a while you learn that

friendship is sanctuary
not shelter
and kisses are presents
not covenants
contracts
promises
profit or pay.
And you know that

a man is only a boy
with more obligations to settle
than dreams left to mortgage
or schemes left to keep them
at bay.

After a while you begin
to build bridges
of mortar and stone,
leaving cracked plank and mud-spit
to tides.
And so you build bridges
to keep yourself dry
to keep yourself safe
from currents crossed
careful as confidences
confided.

And you mourn your defeats
as you celebrate victories,
quiet and quick

carry battle scars
humble as truth.

THE WEDDING POEM

for Jim and Janet

Turn away the silence of the lost
Heart.   There is a music in the soul of
Every love.

Winterfed by passion
Eyes once closed will open
Delicate as
Dawn rose heavy lain against the vine.
It is the moon in spring that feeds the hungry heart,
Now ever-sated. It is the fragrance of a love that
Guides the tongue.

Placed like gift a vow in promise
On the altar of a love is
Evermore the stuff of
Music to the found heart.

Other Books in Print

FOUR FACES OF POETRY
Authors:
>James Edgerton
>Linda Born
>Grant E. Henson
>Rosemary J. Schmidt
>>*Introduction by Dorothy Aust*
>>>Price $10.00 plus $2.00 shipping

CORNERSTONES
Authors:
>Jeanne Heath Heritage
>Elizabeth A. Bernstein
>Jenny M. Stoffle
>Rosemary J. Schmidt
>>*Introduction by Bettye K. Wray*
>>>Price $10.95 plus $2.00 shipping

POEMS OF THE RIVER JUNCTION
Authored by twenty-three Michigan poets.
>>*Introduction by Patrick Pillars*
>>>Price $10.00 plus $2.00 shipping

EVERY LIVING MOMENT and other poetry
Anthology containing the works
>of American, Canadian and Australian poets
>>*Dedicated to John W. Murray, 1918-1992*
>>>Price 12.95 plus $2.00 shipping

Wordsmith Publishing Inc.[TM]
6100 Longmeadow Blvd. S.
Saginaw, MI 48603
517-793-9036

ISBN 0-9628611-7-0 $15.95